Debt Cures®

"They" Don't Want You to Know About

New & Updated

Debt Cures®

*"They" Don't Want You
to Know About*

New & Updated

Debt Cures® "They" Don't Want You to Know About
New & Updated

This edition published by Equity Press, LLC
For information, address:

Debt Cures - New & Updated
PO Box 8508
Pueblo, CO 81008

ISBN 13: 978-0-9819897-6-1

Interior design: The Printed Page, Phoenix, AZ

Manufactured in the United States of America

10 9 8 7 6 5 4 3 2 1

First Version

Contents

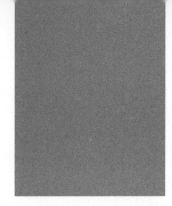

Greetings!

I absolutely loved putting out the first *Debt Cures* book. It was ground breaking and received such great response. There was so much needed information to share with you, because of so much ridiculous garbage happening with the government and the credit card industry and the banks! And, look at us now! What has changed?! The time that has elapsed since that first book has brought us even more ridiculous garbage coming down from the feds and the credit card crooks and the fat cat bankers. So now, here we are again, coming at you with even more much needed information.

Our economy took a nose dive. Crashed and burned. We hit bottom, rock bottom. The depression or the recession or "downturn" or whatever you want to call it left us in a bad state of affairs. The housing market didn't just decline, it fell off a cliff. Unemployment hit the country with a vengeance. Things got tight, really tight. Things got bad. Things got worse. The economy was and is as bad as any time in history.

As much as the government talks about "recovery," most folks have not seen real hard proof of that. The government has come up with all kinds of programs to try to put a band aid on the situation. We're still bleeding.

The first Debt Cures They Don't Want You to Know About was spot on. Around here, we call'em as we see'em and we know our stuff. We launched a monthly newsletter to keep you up to date on all the latest information going on with loans, rates, debts, credit scores, all kinds of money topics that affect your daily life, and we give up-to-the-minute advice on what you can do to stay sane among the idiots.

Knowledge is power. I can never say that enough. We want to give you all the power we possibly can, so here is the next weapon for your arsenal. This book, all updated for you. We will give you, here and now, the latest and best tactics to keep your head above water and how to learn how to float, even if the flood waters are still coming.

The government tries to help, but their programs just aren't cutting it. Their success rate is dismal. The number of folks with no job, the number of people still facing foreclosure, and the amount of hard working American citizens with credit card bills through the roof is still staggering. The economy shows a glimmer of hope every now and then, and then BAM, back into the pit we go.

So dive in to these pages. This book is like the life boat coming to rescue you. You keeping yourself informed is the life jacket. I also see images of bullet proof jackets and six-shooters, but maybe that's too harsh. We don't need to take prisoners. We simply need to stand up for ourselves, our rights, and take our financial matters into our own hands. Thinking the government is going to bail us out is unrealistic. The sinking ship we call the federal government only bails out the corporate big dogs. The little guy is left to sink or swim.

We're strong swimmers, we on the *Debt Cures* team. So are you. Hold on to this book and make sure you get the monthly newsletter.

This book is like the anchor and the monthly newsletter is the GPS system. The newsletter will continue to keep you up to date with all the latest information to guide you, to show you where to steer.

Thanks for your continued support. Thanks for buying my books. Thanks for knowing that the information I give is aimed to help you. The government keeps trying to muddy my name. I've been a target of theirs for years. You all know me as Kevin Trudeau, consumer advocate. I'm the guy who sticks up for you. They know me as Kevin Trudeau, the guy who sticks it to them. They don't like my attitude or my brash disrespect for what goes on in Washington and in corporate boardrooms.

> You taking charge is always the best cure.

Tough.

I love this country. I love my freedom to have my opinion and to express myself. I love that I can point out where things need to be fixed. I am not the only person on this planet who sees flaws in our government and corporate greed. I simply do it loudly and boldly so the feds and the suits want me to shut up.

I'm not shutting up. I am selling books to inform you and to educate you. I also want to engage you, too. You have the power to make changes in your life. You can live better and you do not have to rely on the government to lead the way. You can lead your own path.

I am a messenger. (The government wants to shoot the messenger.) I bring to you what I know. I want to help the hard working citizens of this great land. I don't like abuse. I don't like injustice.

I don't like the way stuff gets done. Or doesn't get done. I want things to be different and this is my way of making a difference.

I am not a lawyer or an accountant or a financial expert. I don't fight in court or sign off on anyone's tax returns. I am simply a hard working citizen of this country and I want to help my fellow man. If that sounds grandiose, so be it. I like calling attention to what needs attention. I have been a whistle blower when needed. That's who I am.

This book is chock full of tips, techniques, and tools to help you get out of debt and help you make some cash too. Opening your eyes to the possibilities is the way to cure your debt.

Times continue to change and we need to continually keep ourselves up to date with the best information and methods available. You taking charge is always the best cure. You need the tools to help. Here you go.

If you have questions about this information as it relates specifically to your detailed personal financial situation, sit down with your tax accountant, financial planner, lawyer, or trusted expert. I am not the expert. I am the collector of information and the messenger of information. Use this information for your best welfare.

This book provides information and research to help you. We, here at the *Debt Cures* team, believe you need to know what goes on in Washington and in the executive offices of the credit card and banking industry. What did I say a few paragraphs ago? Knowledge is power. The more you know, the better you make choices that serve YOU. You are the boss of your life and your finances. You don't need permission to take control of your checkbook or your debt. It's yours. Now is the time. Quit waiting for something to deliver you from the mess. The government has shown that they only make the mess messier.

We at *Debt Cures* appreciate hearing your stories. Let us know how this book helped you. Thank you in advance for that. Let me also say thank you to all who worked hard to make this book possible. A book is a team effort. Thank you, team. And, of course, thank you for reading. This book is dedicated to you.

Introduction

*"It is not the ship so much as the skillful sailing
that assures the prosperous voyage."*
—George William Curtis

This book you hold in your hands is a weapon. Not a weapon of mass destruction. It is a weapon you have for your own good. A weapon to fight off the bad decisions and the greedy ways that come from our nation's capital and from the top offices of some of the richest companies on earth.

The credit card industry and the banking industry have shown over and over in these last few years how out for money they really are. The gloves came off and their greed was raw and exposed. We learned of so much corruption and so many mistakes, and all at the taxpayers' expense.

Use this book as your weapon

This book is the weapon to guard you. It holds knowledge and tools to help you build your financial house from the ground up again. Many feel their financial house has been destroyed these last several years. You can rebuild. You can fortify. You can be strong, no matter what happens.

It is a shame that so many have been affected by the fallout of our government and the greed of the credit card crooks and banking bulldogs. If you took a hit to your financial situation, you are not alone. Millions lost their homes. Millions lost their jobs. Millions faced bankruptcy. Millions of Americans who trusted in the government and in big business. How was that trust returned?

I take a lot of heat for speaking up like this. I've said it before, and I will say it again now, I believe that if more people like me had spoken up, our current economic situation would not be in the state of affairs that it is right now.

> You can be strong no matter what happens.

The government types and the corporate executives tried to give the old song and dance routine. They make up stories and excuses and they withhold facts. They spin, spin, spin. The end result is that the economy crashed and we are left holding the bag.

You are nobody's fool

We are nobody's fool. Yet we pay the price. Our economy is in the dog house. We are no longer a revered super power in the world. The world economy, too, is crumbling in many countries.

The crazy and the lazy and the greedy keep developing new tactics. We put on our armor of knowledge to combat them. You don't have to get mad. You can get even. Simply by taking the reins of your financial power and no longer blindly trusting will save you big bucks and ease your stress.

We can play their game.

We don't need a government bailout. We can bail out our own boat. We don't have to sink in the seas that they try to flood us with. We have information and that equates to power. We have a life boat that we are calling *Debt Cures - New & Updated*.

Debt Cures - New & Updated is information-packed. The economy doesn't seem to be improving, so we can take matters into our hands to improve our own personal economy. The more things change, the more they stay the same. Your grandparents and great-grandparents would advise you to be self-reliant. Good advice.

Don't look to the government for relief

The federal government offers relief packages and only a few actually get that relief. Most Americans are caught in the daily struggle of going to work—for those who have a job—and trying to pay the bills every month while raising kids and worrying about the future of those kids. Doctor bills. Dentist bills. Johnny needs braces. Susie needs glasses. The kids need shoes, and school supplies, and winter coats.

Most Americans are not dealing with issues like whether or not to sell the vacation home in Spain or what to do with the private jet or where to invest that extra million bucks. Most Americans have real problems, real issues, real struggles.

Do you have a mortgage you are struggling to meet each month? Are you facing foreclosure? Do you have credit card bills that seem to get bigger with every passing day? Do you have debt that depresses you? Do you wonder how you are going to make ends meet? Do you have job? Is it a job in your field or are you hauling boxes at Home Depot because it's the place that was hiring?

Things are tough. They have been tough. The government spouts recovery, yet no one is feeling it.

Create your own recovery

There is recovery. It may not come from the government, but it can happen. It can start here, now. Have you heard anyone say that a book has changed their life? Millions do. This book can change yours.

Life changing ideas and information don't usually come from the government, but they do come from books. Like this one. *Debt Cures - New & Updated* offers:

- ✔ Methods to get out of debt.
- ✔ "Magic words" to use to improve your financial situation.
- ✔ Secrets to get FREE money.

The time is now. You have waited long enough. They—the feds, the banks, the corporate suits—have made promises and yet we've seen little real help. It's time to take your financial matters into your own hands. You know who you can trust, and that's YOU. No more waiting for a rescue that will never come. Grab your pride, your integrity, your dignity and climb into the life boat. You can sail your way to financial freedom.

Sail away to a new future

Debt Cures - New & Updated will keep you afloat. It will put the wind back into your sails. They may have pulled the plug and you felt like you were drowning. Your life vest is inflated now. This one book is the gift you can give yourself AND everyone you know who needs relief.

You are no longer being tossed about at sea, bouncing around on the waves with no control and no hope. As you try to keep your head above water, you are tired of seeing the big yachts drive by without even a glance to help you. They keep going, leaving you in the wake. The greedy big boys are losing their steam. You will sail right past them in time.

> ...take financial matters into your own hands.

You are your own skipper. Consider this book your first mate or deck crew. It is that helping hand. Use the methods, tips, and techniques provided in these pages to steer you to smoother waters.

Focus on the big picture

No matter how angry and frustrated I get with the government and the corporate world, I never lose hope for the bigger picture. That's another reason all those corporate guys hate me. I don't play into their fear tactics. I tell it straight. I tell what they are up to and what is not working. They want you to think you need them. I think you should be the one to decide that. Look how much they helped you this far.

The waters may be rough, but you can navigate. The lighthouse is shining. Keep steering toward that. You don't have to launch the torpedoes. A simple weapon like this book is your anchor and your compass. It does not matter the size of your ship, it is the skillful sailing that assures the prosperous voyage. Let *Debt Cures - New & Updated* assist your skillful sailing and help you sail on to a brighter future.

CHAPTER 1

More Knowledge, More Power

"Knowledge is power."
—Francis Bacon

The years have changed. The situation has not.

The first *Debt Cures* book, *Debt Cures They Don't Want You to Know About*, helped so many people. Over three million copies were sold, so that means even more people than that benefited from the book. Every person who bought the book shared some of the ideas with folks they know. Family members in their house, family members outside their home, friends, neighbors, coworkers. When we learn something that helps us, we tell others. It's our human nature. Millions and millions have been helped.

That is amazing. That also tells you how many people are seeking relief.

Soon after that first *Debt Cures* book came out, the economy went to hell in a hand basket, so we came out with a follow-up edition right away to help ease the pain of the crashed economy. It was packed with more tips and tools to ride the wave.

Here we are again

And, here we are now. Who would have believed that the woes of the economy would still be upon us? That too is amazing, and very disappointing. So here we are again, with the latest and best strategies and techniques to help you.

The government and credit industry have been in bed together for years. It's a money game between them and the money is always about them. Helping the American people falls through the cracks.

Some industry insiders, who don't want repercussions for going public, professed what we already know. The laws are written and geared towards making sure people stay in debt and continue on in debt. One insider who feared going on record stated: "Many consumers were taken advantage of by the banking industry that I work for."

That's what I've been saying for years. The financial sector is the biggest contributor to political campaigns. It's a big game to them. Who loses? We do.

Ripoff artists

The federal government, in essence, allows the credit card companies and banks to rip off the American public.

They want money, plain and simple. One banking president once said something to the effect, "We make most of our money from the people who are the most desperately in need of credit cards and loans."

The banks are not there to serve your needs. They are there to serve THEIR needs. Their need for more and more of your money.

Does that make headlines?

The news used to be rampant with stories of foreclosures, housing market decline, unemployment, and all the ways our economy has tanked. Then it became old news. The headlines went away because there was nothing new to say.

Same old news

We STILL have foreclosures, housing market decline, and unemployment. We STILL have an economy that's in the toilet. We STILL have an inept government and greedy politicians, corporate and banking executives.

We STILL have a sluggish recovery. We STILL have a faulty foundation created by government attempts to bailout. We STILL have historic highs and lows, neither for the good of our citizens.

Record high unemployment. Record high foreclosures. Record high bankruptcies. Record low interest rates. Record low housing prices. Record low trust in a real economic recovery.

> The headlines went away because there was nothing new to say.

We STILL need *Debt Cures*. Ask and you shall receive. Here you go. The all-new, updated for the current times edition. Years go by and yet, wow, some things do not change. The muddled mess of bureaucracy. The muddled mess of government programs. The muddled mess of abusive practice by banks and credit card companies.

A long and enduring crisis

In the last *Debt Cures* book, I wrote: "The economy has NEVER been like this. What we are going through now is a once-in-a-century kind of crisis. Never in our lifetime—or any time before that—has the nation experienced financial crashes of this nature, like we have been going through lately."

This "once-in-a-century crisis" has turned out to be a very long and enduring kind of crisis. I am not a history buff, but it seems that even the Great Depression had a better turn around than what we are experiencing.

This has been a crash and tumble that kept tumbling. And tumbling. And tumbling. The fallout kept falling. The upturn may have glimmered and sparked, but then it sputtered and puttered to nothing. Nothing really happened. Nothing really changed. The business as usual is lingering doubt and lingering turmoil and lingering disillusion.

It's time for winds of change.

I am no psychic or seer or fortune teller. I call what I see. I tell it like I see it. I saw back in 2007 with the first *Debt Cures* They Don't Want You to Know About that we were headed for a fall. My critics purport that I like to make noise and bluster, well, I did make noise and I do stir folks up. I also hit a bulls-eye. This economic disaster could have been avoided. That's what really gets my ire up.

America is still getting screwed

I said in plain language for everyone to read that the government regulations are on the side of the corporate powers-that-be, and that the American citizen is getting screwed. I stated that the fat cat bankers and the credit card institutions were greedy and borderline corrupt and that the government looked the other way.

Maybe I am a psychic.

Or maybe it is just plain obvious. Look at all that has come to light. Some are indeed "borderline" corrupt and some long passed that border into flat-out corrupt. Look at all the fraud cases and mishandling of affairs. Who gets screwed? The average Joe. The big dogs settle out of court and don't make big splashy news for their screw ups.

It's the normal guy who gets crushed. It's the people just like you, and all those that you know, who do everything you can to make your bills and do what is right. The other guys, the greedy execs, stomp all over you. You are the one trying to do what is right and you are the one getting put down.

Doesn't have to stay that way.

Abusive practices continue

The abusive practices and the sloppy methods of the credit card companies and banks have been brought to the forefront. There have been lawsuits and settlements and they are having to pay. Yet, their ways are still creating havoc. For everything they are called on the carpet for, they go back to their evil laboratories and concoct new ways to put the screws to the taxpayers.

They get in trouble for an abusive practice and yet they do not change their ways. They try to make nice in that one area where they got busted and yet they are always creating ways to get more money out of the public.

The lending practices and the basic policies and procedures of the big banks and credit companies have come under scrutiny. For good reason. And they have not passed with flying colors. Their antics and abuse is a crying shame. However, they express no shame and we are the ones left crying.

...big banks and credit companies have come under scrutiny.

It is the public who carries the burden. It is the public who gets screwed time and time again. The average citizen gets taken advantage of and the big dogs get away with it. Over and over. The cycle repeats.

The government speaks of new regulations and watchdogs and keeping an eye on the industry. Yet it still keeps happening.

Records we do not want

Record numbers of people have lost their homes. Many of those foreclosures could have been avoided. Record numbers of people have lost their jobs. Record numbers of bankruptcies have occurred. Record numbers of businesses have been forced to close.

The government speaks of aid and recovery programs. The primary ones getting this aid and recovery money are the very ones who created and caused this mess. The big money corporations and banks are the ones getting the government money. The big money corporations and banks were the ones who set this whole chain of events in motion. Their greed, their corruption, their practices, started the avalanche.

They have spent years taking advantage of the average consumer and when their greed backfired on them, it caused this collapse of our economy. And, what happened? They are the ones to get government money, not the people who have been hurt the most.

What's wrong?

It's a warped system.

With the record number of people needing help, the banks slammed their doors in their faces. The banks created the struggle and when the average Joe asked for help, the banks said no. The banks wield the power and they do it arrogantly and unfairly. They do it selfishly.

Do you know anyone getting a good loan with good terms these days? Are the banks easy to work with? Tough times continue. The banks used to be in the business of lending money. Now their only motive is to make money, hand over fist, any way they can.

It is maddening. If the big banks would have applied sound business practices all along, we would not be in this predicament and we would not be stuck in the mud that came sliding down on us in this avalanche of their mistakes. They created the mess, yet they are not the ones still down slogging in the mud. We are.

Equally maddening is how they deny culpability. They play innocent. They only worry about themselves and their next dime. They would steal that dime from a baby if they could. There has been no evidence or admission of personal or corporate responsibility. It has only been a saga of "poor me."

Stop the madness

The banks and the lenders and the credit card companies are not sweet and innocent. They did not make innocent mistakes. They make calculated decisions and their driving goal was how much money they could make.

When the walls came tumbling down, they were the ones crying for a bailout. The big dogs and the rich fat cats were the ones that created this financial nightmare and they were the ones cowering, sucking their thumbs, whining, "Help us."

They never owned up to screwing millions of people and yet the federal government gave them billions of dollars. What kind of deal is that?!

How many people do they get to rip off? Obviously, millions. How do they get punished for it? Not at all. Instead, they get billions of dollars of government money.

The system is twisted, biased, unfair, and wrong.

What does the government tell all the folks who lost their homes? We gave that money to the banks.

> The system is twisted, biased, unfair and wrong.

What does the government tell all the folks who lost their jobs? We gave that money to the banks.

What does the government tell all the folks who faced bankruptcy? We gave that money to the banks.

It's a tale as old as time. Greed, corruption, the old boys network. Lies, deceit, and misplaced trust.

The roller coaster ride continues

It's been quite a roller coaster ride these past several years since the last *Debt Cures* book came out. That tale is still part of the fabric of our current culture. The big boys bellowed for a bailout. Banks, credit card companies, automakers. All ready and willing to take a government handout. And, money the government does give. The deficit is in the trillions and the federal government has no concept of a balanced budget. They give money and it sure seems they give money to the wrong folks. Did you hear that even the porn industry asked for a government bailout when the economy tanked?! How that industry was affected I have no idea.

The economy tanked, plain and simple. People accused me of exaggeration in the first book and yet look at us now. Exaggerate? I'd say I was more of a prophet.

Greed and corruption, no exaggeration there. Lies and abuse, no exaggeration there. Deceit and dollars, no exaggeration there. Who got screwed? The average, hard-working American citizen. No exaggeration there.

We must return to self-reliance

Is the American dream just a sham now? No exaggeration there. Do people work a lot harder these days for less? No exaggeration there. Did the corruption of corporate ethics create crisis for all? No exaggeration there.

Do I also know the resilience of the American consumer? Hell yes. No exaggeration there. Do I also know that we can take matters into our own hands and come out on top? Hell yes. No exaggeration there. Do I know that the tactics in this book are part of the tools of the battle? Hell yes. No exaggeration there.

Our forefathers taught us to believe in our great country and to believe in ourselves. Self-reliance and self-trust are steadfast values. No matter what good things or foolish things the government does, the buck really does stop here. You are the boss of you, you are the CEO of you, you are the president of you.

We know the government is not going to give a bailout to the American people. The government has been in bed with the others for too long. They're warm and comfortable. They are also tangled in the webs of deceit.

We can create our own bailout. We can make our own changes. We can employ the tactics and methods in these pages to create our own economic recovery.

A lot has changed since the first *Debt Cures* was printed, and much has stayed the same. The economy and financial situation of the world will always color your individual world. Keep knowledge as your weapon. When you are informed, you are armed and at the ready.

You will have the tools

Use these strategies and tools to relieve your debt. Stay current and up to date. Keep this book on the shelf with the other *Debt Cures*. Subscribe to the monthly newsletter. Keep adding to your collection of the best and most useful tools for today's world.

It is always my pleasure to bring this information to you. To reveal the latest and best strategies, as well as continuing to expose the secrets of the credit industry is what fulfills me. The thrill is the information and how it helps people.

It is my never ending motto that the truth has to be exposed, and the American people absolutely have to be aware of what the United States federal government, the banks, and the credit card companies are doing, and not doing.

So much has changed and so much has stayed the same. And, so much has even gotten worse.

Credit card reform acts were put in place. What happened? As some fees became regulated, the banks created more fees. Some banks and credit card companies were investigated for their abusive practices. When they got in trouble for one thing, they would behave in that arena for a while, all the while misbehaving elsewhere. On and on it goes. One thing comes to light, while a million others are swept under the rug or ignored.

Banks were sloppy and abusive in their foreclosure proceedings. The spotlight was shifted there, which only served to slow the process, not stop the process. Foreclosures still keep coming. And with such, home values have continued to plummet.

Jobs are still hard to come by. Selling your house for what it was valued at in 2009 is a joke. So many people are underwater in their mortgage that even grade schoolers understand that term now. "Our house is not worth what we paid for it. We could sell it today and not have enough money to pay what we owe on it." Short sales used to be a once-in-a-while event. Now they are commonplace.

Face it, the economy is still down

The economy has not improved for years. We have been holding "steady" here for way too long.

It's time to demand change. The election promise of 2008 spoke of change. What have we really seen? Change?

Any change for the better?

Are you better off than you were?

What was promised in the election of 2012? What have we received? Are you liking this kind of change created by this administration?

It's time to be demanding

Demand answers. Demand the truth. Demand to know what goes on in Washington. Demand to know what goes on in the banks and corporate credit card headquarters. Demand to know what they tell their employees. Demand to know their practices. Demand to know your rights.

> It's time to demand change.

I demand such information. And, I share it with you.

This is your country. This is your home. You are the king (or queen) of your castle. You are not a peasant and will not be treated as such.

This is the United States of American and everyone should play by the same rules. Big corporate rich man or hard working blue collar man. Same rules.

I'm no stranger to that world. I have been in closed door conferences in some fine corporate boardrooms. I have seen the wealth, and the attitudes, and the arrogance, and the disregard and the greed.

You know what. They can be wealthy and arrogant and have an attitude of disregard and be downright greedy. So be it. As long as they play by the same rules as the average citizen, I'm okay. They can stink up the room all they want with attitude and arrogance, as long as they play by the same rules, it doesn't matter. ·

The American Dream

We all want wealth. It's the American Dream. Wealth is good. Money is wonderful. You deserve money and wealth, too. We all do. You can be a corporate big wig or a small town business owner or you can be a teacher, a preacher, a baker, a factory worker, a dancer, a tailor, it does not matter.

This is America. We play by the same rules. We all can get wealthy.

Seriously, we all can get wealthy. This still is America and this still is the land of dreams. Things are pretty messed up, but the inherent ability to live your dreams has not been squandered by the greedy bastards.

YOU can make money

The ones in power are the ones who get sidetracked by their greed and their loss of principles. You can be an entrepreneur in this great country and you can make money. You can be rich. You can be wealthy. It's how you go about it. Do you want to be like the corrupt big dogs or do you want to have plenty of money and have self-respect too. You can.

Attitude. Arrogance. Greed. Corruption. Abusive practices. That's the difference between the people in power that are making the rules and those who are in the real world struggling from day to day to pay the bills and make ends meet. The hard-working honest folks in our country know that there is a little something called character and ethics and not taking advantage of the little guy.

There is also a whole other world out there though, the "big boys" of the credit industry, the banking industry, and the lobbyists and the senators who make the laws and regulations. The playbook they carry is their own and they think they are the only ones who get to play by their rules, because they are the ones who are making up their rules.

Wrong.

You, the hard working, tax paying citizen of this country, are demanding the answers. You demand the truth. Keep demanding.

We exposed a lot of the games and unfair practices of the government, the banks, and the credit industry in the first *Debt Cures* books. Now millions of people have started paying attention to what is going on in Washington and with the credit lending industry. We have seen some regulations and some change and some truth come to light.

Stand in your power

When you demand the truth, you get answers.

Stand in your power. You may not be a CEO of a corporation, but you have power. You don't have to take the abuse. You don't have to stay in the dark. You don't have to accept being treated unfairly.

Always remember that knowledge is power. The more you know, the more power in your arsenal. The purpose of this updated book is to give you updated power. More amps, more juice, more ammunition.

Ready. Aim. Fire!

CHAPTER 2

Real Life Success Stories

"Always bear in mind that your own resolution to succeed is more important than any other."
—Abraham Lincoln

What about you? Have you made up your own mind that you want to succeed? You can, you know. It does not have to be hard. People tend to overcomplicate things. We make life harder than it has to be.

None of the solutions presented in the *Debt Cures* methods here are hard or complicated. Nobody needs a degree or to go back to night school or to hire a translator to decipher any kind of code. You don't need to hire a tutor and you don't need to know how to spell or do complex math. You can do basic reading and writing and use a calculator, that's all you need and you've got it made. You can use your mouth to speak up. That's key. You can learn to stay silent when that matters, too.

Think you can handle those simple things?

I do.

Simple is sufficient

That's what this book is about, telling you what to do, what not to do, when and why. We tell you the how to do it all. It is laid out simple and easy. I don't like to confuse people. I like to tell it straight.

Debt Cures They Don't Want to You to Know About, and this updated version, are geared for you, the normal guy trying to make it in this world.

Many people think that only "other people" get out of debt. Only "other people" become wealthy. Only "other people" have a great life.

Who do you think those other people are? They are people just like you!

They wised up to the ways of the world. They stopped believing all the garbage they were fed by the government and the credit card creeps. They started sticking up for themselves. They started reading books like this and doing something about their situation.

Real people, real results

People like Ruth D. know that you can use methods like those discussed in *Debt Cures* and get out of debt. Ruth and her family got out of debt to the tune of $2.1 MILLION.

That's a lot of dough.

Her husband got injured and could not work. Things were tough. They knew they had to do something. Ruth said the debt was stressful. "It's a huge amount of pressure. It can cause a person to go into depression and despair."

So many people think it's impossible to overcome that kind of debt. It's very possible. Like Ruth says, "You can have new ways of thinking, you can absolutely conquer the debt. We started small and we eliminated the cable bill, the coffee stops, the expensive haircuts."

Ruth and her husband employed methods that you will read about here, like accelerating the payment on credit cards and negotiating. They sold stuff, including a vacation home. They were systematic. They liquidated their home and their second home, and they paid off all the medical bills, the doctor bills, two school loans and both cars are paid for. It was over two million in debt.

Can you imagine?

They proclaim: "It's just the hugest relief not to have to owe or worry about money and paying bills and things like that. One of the beautiful things is that we get to spend more time with family. The things that bring people happiness, we get to do more of that. Which is spend time with family, do community quality time, travel and just hang out with the family."

Do you want to be like Ruth or do you want to be like "other people?"

Get off the couch

Other people sit on their butts on the couch and think that something or someone will come along and make it all better. That's what "other people" do.

You are among the REAL PEOPLE who eliminate their debt and embrace the path to wealth.

We get letters from real people with real success stories. This stuff, these *Debt Cures* methods, is good stuff. It's great stuff. It works.

> So make a resolution right now that you want to succeed.

Simply follow the steps outlined in the chapters, and you (yes, you) can get out of debt and start making money. Creating wealth is just as much fun as getting out of debt, right?

Keeping your money in your wallet and out of their greedy, grubby fists is a success. So make a resolution right now that you want to succeed. Make up your mind that you are just as smart as any banker or loan officer or creditor or collection creep. You do not have to fall for their scare tactics.

I want you to know that you have what it takes to get out of debt. Believe it.

Start feeling confident about your success story. Start to imagine it now. Start to write your thank you letter now, before it even happens.

Always remember that knowledge is power and that you are mighty strong, armed with knowledge. This book is your weapon.

I have been attacked, so I know what it's like to feel pressure and stress. I have had my share of hard knocks and I have had way many more successes. I keep reading and learning and improving. I keep bettering myself. I keep arming myself with knowledge. It is my armor, my protection, my weapon.

Never give up

I don't give up. I don't back down. I fight for what I know is right. I fight for the average American citizen who needs to know what to do when facing big debt and big fear.

Debt Cures methods work. They relieve your debt and your stress. These methods help people live better lives.

I could fill an entire book with all the testimonials that I have received. There are stories that make you laugh and stories that make you cry. It would not matter. My critics would not be satisfied. They are always looking for ways to attack me. They probably always will. I am getting used to it by now.

The stories are here to serve a purpose—to help you. You, too, may be a doubter or a skeptic. You want to believe that this stuff can work for you. It helps to read other real life people stories because they, too, doubted and wondered if their lives could change.

We will give you a handful of stories to be an inspiration for you. Let them light your candle of hope.

Be inspired

Lolita writes: *"Just wanted to let you know how much I appreciate your advice in your book. I cannot put the book down from Day 1. I started reading the book on the night that I got it from the mail and I went into action the very next day. I called my credit card company with the highest interest rate, to request a reduction in my rate. My latest statement showed a whopping 30.10% APR! The customer service person who initially answered the phone was of no help, so I insisted on talking to a Manager or Supervisor.*

I made the same request to the Supervisor and he put me on hold for a minute. When he came back, he said he has reinstated my interest rate to 11.66% (from 30.10%)!!!! I tried to be calm, said thank you and asked him if the rate reduction will be effective in the next month's statement cycle. To my surprise (again!), he said, "No, it will be effective immediately." And, there's more! He continued to say, "I even credited you for an interest refund of about $87.00 right now."

Wow, I felt the power on my very first attempt!"

POWER. You, too, will feel the power.

That's what we want. The power back in YOUR hands.

Be inspired

Nanette writes: *"I would like to "Thank You" for a wonderful book and the great advice and debt education. I have since negotiated three of my credit cards (two down to ZERO PERCENT "0%" and 1 to TEN PERCENT "10%!!!).*

This was the best investment I have ever purchased—not to mention the techniques explained really work!! Thank you so much, Kevin!!

You are very welcome.

Be inspired

Jim wrote: *"When I got to my Discover Card statements I noticed that I had late payment fees and a very high interest rate. I called them on Tuesday afternoon around 1:30 or 2:00 p.m. (I mention this because I had very little wait time on hold.). I asked to have my interest rate lowered, which the person did, and I asked for my late fee back, which she did.*

I feel great because instead of losing money, I made money. It took me maybe 20 minutes to make the call and I saved $39.00 in late fees plus whatever the lower interest rate was, that works out to over $117.00 per hour!"

One phone call. Big bucks saved. That is what you learn in these pages.

Be inspired

Dorothy wrote: *"After reading the first fifty pages of Debt Cures I was able to cut our interest rates on our two highest credit cards ($19,000 and $8,000) from 29% to 3%— saving us thousands. Thank you, Kevin!"*

Again, my pleasure.

Be inspired

Lalla wrote: *"In cleaning up my credit reports and increasing FICO scores, I was able to get two of the credit reporting agencies to delete a negative item."*

Bravo.

Be inspired

Pat wrote: *"A financial burden has been lifted off my shoulders! Improved my credit score over 100 points! Thank You, Kevin!"*

Love it.

Are you tired of reading letters like this? I'm not.

Be inspired

Arjun wrote: *"I have credit card debt and student loans and not getting by on what I make now out of school. I called my CitiCard and told her my whole long story. I explained that I would have to file bankruptcy because I cannot pay my bills and I want to offer them some kind of pay off. We talked for a long time. She explained she could not take a settlement offer, but she could offer me an introductory rate of 0% for the next 12 months. I asked if that was the best she could do and she said yes, and then offered to transfer me to someone who could talk to me about a repayment plan. I am excited to be getting back on track!"*

The *Debt Cures* track is an exciting track indeed.

Be inspired

Parker wrote: *"A year ago I had my third back surgery. It did not go well and not only am I in more pain than before, but I lost my health with a bipulmonary embolism and pneumonia, then I lost my income, then I lost my wife. On the brink of bankruptcy and having my first mortgage jump to $2,400.00 a month, I was desperate.*

Without health, without a job and nothing more than $100.00 in my bank, I thought all was lost. Then I called my mortgage holder. I spoke candidly and used the information in your book.

I got the phone call today from my first mortgage holder that my payment was being lowered from $2,400.00 to $1,375.00 a month. I just got more than $1,000.00 off a month and all this without a job, money in the bank and being disabled.

You have given me some hope that I can hold on to my house and make some stability for my children.

Thank you for making this information available."

Hope. That's what everyone needs. You, too, can have hope that your life can change for the better.

Be inspired

Marc wrote: *"I was able to change my interest rate on my Credit Card from 11.24% to a wonderful 1.9% just by using the information I learned while reading thus far. I can't wait to see what I will learn next throughout the rest of the book!"*

You can start applying what you learn right away. You don't even have to get through the whole book to start seeing money.

Deanna wrote: *"Your information has absolutely changed my life."*

Thank you.

This information can change your life, too.

You need to know that these methods and strategies can work for you, too. These letters mention some of the tactics and strategies that you may not know yet. That's what this book is for—to clue you in. If some of the words are not familiar, hang tight. The following pages will tell you what you need to know and it will all make sense.

Readers from all over the country have poured in their heartfelt gratitude and success stories, thanks to *Debt Cures* books and newsletters. You can be among the real life success stories, too.

We love it, too

Lori wrote: *Hello! We purchased the* Debt Cures *book and love it! We have learned so much about the lending industry and feel our eyes are now "wide open" where previously we didn't have a clue!*

Yes! Eyes wide open! That is the purpose of this book. People need to open their eyes to what is going on all around us. Stop being so naïve and trusting. When we let that happen, they—the fat cats with the power—can get away with ripping you off! Is that what you want?

Of course not!

You too can live again

Jocelyn wrote: *"I would love to tell my story. I would like to tell someone that you don't have to settle or take it from those harassing creditors.*

It is all over when you buy the book. It will teach you how to clean up and keep your credit. It has so helped me and my family.

I can live again!"

Did you catch what she said? "I can live again!" Give that a great big hell yes! That is a powerful statement.

When a person feels trapped with mountains of debt and the collectors are calling and harassing, it can be a nightmare. The whole family can get dragged down. So many people do not know that there are ways to defeat the overbearing collection rats. Well, not anymore!

The methods you will learn will help you live again. If you are experiencing the anxiety and hassles that these folks did, this is the book for you. Real life solutions that can work for you too!

The power comes in knowing what to do and how to begin the process. That is the most common complaint that I hear when people tell me about their debt troubles: "Kevin, I am so overwhelmed; I don't even know where to begin."

Straight talk

That is why I give it to you straight. No mumbo-jumbo, no fancy jargon, and no fine print. It's all right here in easy-to-understand English. Step by step, you can take back control of your finances and even more important, you can take back your life.

There is power in numbers and the more people who are educated about what is really going on will make it harder for the credit card executives and their buddies in Washington to continue with their deceptive ways. Share the *Debt Cures* information with your family, friends, neighbors, coworkers, and college students. Share these methods with everyone!

Robert wrote: *"I wish I would have known these techniques sooner."*

Yes. We know. So many folks don't know the deal. Let us all agree to educate as many people as we can. The sooner, the better.

Too many folks have been taken advantage of and are paying too much money to the creditors. Let's get money back in our wallets again. We want the whole world to know what the credit and banking industry does so we don't fall prey to their schemes ever again.

There has been over the years, and still going on, a lot of negative talk about me. Big deal.

I've got a reputation and I don't back down from it. I am one of the guys the feds and corporations love to go after. I don't play their games and I'm not afraid to blow the lid off what is really going on.

> Step by step, you can take back control of your finances...

I've been "in the know" for several years. I have been behind closed doors and heard the bragging. I've heard the banking top dogs exclaim that not only are they making outrageous dollars, they are making "obscene profits!"

They were proud to be making obscene profits off of the hard working American. That makes me sick. We all want to make a profit from an honest day's work, but these guys are looking to make an obscene profit any way they can.

Bullies don't scare us

I have already taken on some powerhouses in the government in past programs and books. They don't scare me. They can bully me. They can sue me. They can threaten all kinds of stuff. I just keep on.

No one likes the guy who tries to expose the truth when the truth means money. That is the bottom line. It all comes back to money. The credit lending industry wants your money. And, the government is right there with them. So, of course, they all would much prefer that I keep my mouth shut and stop writing these kinds of books.

Tough.

I think your money is yours and you need to be educated. Class is in session and let me be your teacher.

People write all the time and say things like: *I am finding out things that I did not know before and I am so glad that I got the book.*

I know that you will be glad you got the book, too.

Because my reputation preceded me, there were people lined up and ready to rip apart *Debt Cures They Don't Want You to Know About.* From the greed and connections and deceit of our country's drug companies to the weight loss industry to the financial wheeler dealers, whistle blower is what I am. I make no apologies. Somebody has to expose the real situation.

The critics wanted to attack me, and they couldn't do it. The *Debt Cures* books, all my books, hold water.

Good reviews

I don't have to make up stuff when the truth is so much more compelling than any fiction could be. The scams of the industry are real and the practical applications for your life are real. This review is from the world of internet blogs where there are folks who wanted to take aim and fire at me. Yet they read the book and realized it was good. Kudos to them.

Let's share from an unaffiliated "*Debt Cures* Review" blog—they wanted to cream me, but ended up complimenting the book.

> Great Book! It's got all the information you need organized nicely in one place. You can probably spend years trying to weed through tons of good and bad information and never feel confident you're getting all the information you need.
>
> Kevin Trudeau's book is an easy read and packed full of

information that WILL help you. Trudeau is one of my heroes for his bravery in exposing different scam industries and he's doing it again with Debt Cures.

With all the negativity and the opposition that I get, I get more gratitude than anything. That is what I focus on. Yes, I am attacked. I am also thanked.

One reader wrote in: *I applaud Kevin Trudeau's fight against... the credit and bank institutes, and for letting the American people know the truth and allowing US to make informed decisions about our financial health.*

Know the truth

> ...we can make informed decisions...

We all need to know the truth so we can make informed decisions about every area of our life. Financial burdens cause stress and stress is the number one health plague in our nation. Doctors proclaim that most disease is caused by stress. What causes stress for most people? Paying their bills!

It's a vicious cycle.

Get the debt and the money under control, you get less stress and life rolls along better in every way. If people can get out of the burden of debt, a weight is lifted and the body experiences it on every level. Learning about your financial affairs and how to alleviate debt AND create more wealth is a major factor in your overall quality of life.

Money talks. Money makes you feel better, in every way. That is, when you know how to hang on to money and not pay it out to lenders and creditors.

Strategy works

Ready to get learning?

This book of strategies is for you to apply right here, right now. You can save thousands too.

- ✔ Robert got his credit card interest rates lowered;

- ✔ Cathy reduced her monthly payments by hundreds of dollars;

- ✔ Jalene had old debt deleted from her credit report in 24 hours;

- ✔ John saved himself $2,000 before he even finished reading the whole book;

- ✔ Randolph saved $2,500 immediately;

- ✔ Francois got rid of ALL his debt!

- ✔ Sylvia got her interest rates lowered and credit lines increased;

- ✔ Pat improved her credit score over 100 points;

- ✔ Jim had late fees removed and interest rate lowered;

- ✔ Lolita had her interest rate reduced 20%;

- ✔ Vendel & Glen got their interest rate lowered from 29.75% to 5.75%;

I could give you testimonials all day.

AP wrote: *We read the book and used one of the tools in the book and we are now credit card debt free. We are saving over $1,000.00 a month by using this tool. Thank you, Kevin, for this book. We are not only credit card debt free but we are also stress free!!*

Are you stress free?

Do you want to be? Who doesn't?

Besides all the letters of thanks, I also get the letters of thanks and "I wish I would have known all this earlier."

No more delays for you. The time to learn and do is now. It's game time. You do not have to suffer any more. You do not have to be trapped in the downward spiral of debt.

You can know all this stuff now. There will be many success stories in the upcoming pages, too.

If you do not want the government and the credit card companies to keep pilfering from your pockets, let's go.

Game on.

CHAPTER 3

Game On

"The best defense is a good offense."

So much spin has occurred during the time between the *Debt Cures* books. The Bailout Edition was released in 2009, as we were entering into the first term of the Obama administration.

A lot has happened.

Now we are entering the second term. How do you feel?

Debtor prison

How do you feel about debtors' prison? It used to be something out of an old Dickens' novel. Getting thrown in jail for not paying your debts dates back to centuries-ago London and even as far back as Roman times. It seems to be occurring now, too.

Back in 1830, folks in Boston were tossed in jail for debts as low as a dollar. That's about twenty to thirty bucks in today's dollars. Outrageous then. Outrageous now.

We didn't think it applied to modern times. The times they are a-changing.

One Missouri woman had a $425 payday loan and ended up in jail. The St. Louis Post-Dispatch reported in 2012, yes, recent times, that arrests based on debts are not uncommon. This gals' mom had to post $1,250 to get her out after three horrible days in a local jail.

The payday loan places and finance companies are using the jails as a way to get money out of folks. What they do is get a civil judgment on someone who owes them money. The debtor is then called in for an examination in civil court.

If the debtor does not show up, the creditor's lawyer asks the court for an order to arrest the person. Arrest. Jail.

The courts are allowing it. Not in all states, but some.

Jail time

It was quite a scam for some collectors. They would send notices requesting repeated court appearances. If you failed to appear, you could be arrested. The rules have changed a tiny bit. Instead of mail, now the court order has to be given in person to the household, to someone over the age of 14.

Can you imagine? Someone shows up at the door and gives your teenager a letter that he forgets to give you. You don't show up in court because you don't see the letter. You get arrested and thrown in jail. Why? Because you owed somebody four hundred bucks.

Talk about abusive practices.

One man was arrested and handcuffed in front of his children. He was thrown in jail, strip-searched, and sprayed for lice. He spent two nights in jail before being released. His "crime" was that he owed $1,500 to a loan company. He knew he owed the debt but had no idea he was being sued or that he was in "contempt of court" as he had never received the letters or notices.

Debtor's prison is not just something out of the history books or novels.

NPR reports: "More than a third of all states now allow borrowers who don't pay their bills to be jailed, even when debtor's prisons have been explicitly banned by state constitutions. A report by the American Civil Liberties Union found that people were imprisoned even when the cost of doing so exceeded the amount of debt they owed." (Source: http://readersupportednews.org/off-site-news-section/255-justice/8929-debtors-prisons-thousands-jailed-in-us-for-bailing-on-bills.)

In Kansas City, one man ended up in jail after missing just one payment on his furniture. The Federal Trade Commission received more than 140,000 complaints related to debt collection in 2010, and they've taken ten debt collection agencies to court for their practices in the past three years.

We'll see how it all plays out.

They'll do anything

There have been thousands and thousands of arrest warrants for debt related cases. Legal aid attorneys state what we already know: Debt collectors will do anything, harshly and aggressively, to get money out of people.

This NPR report also states what we already know. Debt collection is a lucrative business. The collection creep industry is expected to grow over 25% in the next three years. And, this economy is in recovery?

A CBS news report says the same: "Although the U.S. abolished debtors' prisons in the 1830s, more than a third of U.S. states allow the police to haul people in who don't pay all manner of debts, from bills for health care services to credit card and auto loans." (Source: http://finance.yahoo.com/news/jailed-for--280--the-return-of-debtors--prisons.html.)

> ...thousands of arrest warrants for debt related cases.

Technically, debtors aren't arrested for nonpayment, but rather for failing to respond to court hearings, pay legal fines, or otherwise showing "contempt of court" in connection with a creditor lawsuit.

A 2010 report by the American Civil Liberties Union that focused on only five states—Georgia, Louisiana, Michigan, Ohio, and Washington—found that people were being jailed at "increasingly alarming rates" over legal debts. Cases ranged from a woman who was arrested four separate times for failing to pay $251 in fines and court costs related to a fourth-degree misdemeanor conviction, to a mentally ill juvenile jailed by a judge over a previous conviction for stealing school supplies.

The sad truth

Every state seems to show a surge in arrest warrants based on debt collection issues. They don't all result in jail time, but the fact that this practice is on the rise is very alarming. The FTC says they are aware, but they are being mum about what, if any, investigation is being done to stop the abuse.

According to the ACLU report: "The sad truth is that debtors' prisons are flourishing today, more than two decades after the Supreme Court prohibited imprisoning those who are too poor to pay their legal debts. In this era of shrinking budgets, state and local governments have turned aggressively to using the threat and reality of imprisonment to squeeze revenue out of the poorest defendants who appear in their courts."

Ain't that America?

Besides this nonsense, and all the hurricanes and natural disasters that have occurred, we experienced more disasters on the home front in regard to our economy. The foreclosure fiasco kept spiraling downward. Millions and millions of homes were foreclosed. Every year, millions more.

Staggering numbers

Take a look at the numbers.

- ✔ 2007 1.2 million foreclosure filings; 2.2 million foreclosures
- ✔ 2008 2.3 million foreclosures filings; 3 million foreclosures
- ✔ 2009 2.9 million foreclosures filings; 3.4 million foreclosures
- ✔ 2010 3.5 million foreclosures filings; 3.8 million foreclosures
- ✔ 2011 3.5 million foreclosures filings; 3.9 million foreclosures
- ✔ 2012 2.3 million foreclosures filings; 2.6 million foreclosures

Those are the stats provided by RealtyTrac, Federal Reserve, and Equifax. The actual numbers for 2013 are not available as we go to press, yet the numbers for 2012 appear to show a sign of hope. After five years of foreclosures trending on a crazy marked increase, it is reassuring to see that the numbers are easing down.

Yet look at the big picture. We still have over two million foreclosures and over two million new filings. That is still too many people losing their homes. No one should be losing their homes if things were handled properly.

But things were not handled properly and the economic situation got drearier and drearier. It was not just foreclosures going crazy.

State today

More than two million Americans filed for bankruptcy in 2005. That was a record year because the law was then changed to make it more difficult for folks to file bankruptcy. A lot of folks filed before the changes came into place. The rationale for the new regulation was that people were filing bankruptcy to get out of paying their debts. The government, in all its wisdom, decided to make changes to the rules and regulations so that folks could not use bankruptcy as an easy out.

The onslaught of the depressed economy hit and Americans were hit hard. Many folks had no other option. Even with the tight requirements in place to file bankruptcy now, record numbers of people continued to do so.

Although filings dropped after the Bankruptcy Abuse Prevention and Consumer Protection Act of 2005 (BAPCPA) took effect, bankruptcies have grown steadily every year since. 2011 was the first calendar year to show a decrease in total filings since 2006. Accurate stats for 2013 are not released as we go to press. Estimates are roughly about the same as for 2012.

Again, take a look at the numbers:

- ✔ 2007 850,000 bankruptcies
- ✔ 2008 1.1 million
- ✔ 2009 1.4 million
- ✔ 2010 1.5 million
- ✔ 2011 1.4 million
- ✔ 2012 1.1 million

Records are made to be broken, so they say, and we keep breaking them. Not the kind of records we want to be breaking.

Unemployment has also shown record high numbers in these years. Unemployment stats by the Bureau of Labor Statistics are tracked monthly. They may fluctuate a percentage point or so from month to month, but the overall yearly average is about the same as what we show here. We'll recite the numbers as of October (the last month we have available for 2013 at press time) for each year to show the overall pattern.

- 2007 4.7%
- 2008 6.5%
- 2009 10.0%
- 2010 9.5%
- 2011 8.9%
- 2012 8.1%
- 2013 7.3%

Unemployment dipped in 2007 and then roared back and has not really subsided. The worst of 2009 was the high point, yet the numbers still range around 7% or 8% for every month in 2012 and 2013.

Too high

Many people project the actual unemployment numbers are higher than what the statistics show because there are many people who are not employed that are not counted in these figures. Even so, the numbers here still show too many people without a job.

Way too many.

Why all the numbers, stats and figures quoted here?

Simply to show that the economy has nosedived, and it is not going up or even really leveling out just yet. Look at those numbers. See much promise in there? Is this what you call recovery?

How many years do we have to take this garbage?

President Obama was elected in November 2008 promising "change." Yep. We got change. Now is not the time or place to discuss all that happened in the four years of that administration, (maybe later), but suffice to say, change is not always good. Time will tell what becomes of these next four years.

> Too many people without a job.

George Bush once said: "We believe the American people can spend their money better than the government can spend it."

Hell yes. The American people can spend their money better than the clowns in Washington can. No one needs to tell us that, former president or not. The bozo brigade in Washington is still up to tricks and still make poor decisions when it comes to spending our money. Bailouts? Did we see any of that money?

How's your wallet?

I think everyone got a little check four years ago for a couple hundred bucks. Did that save homes? Did that prevent bankruptcy? Did that prevent foreclosure? Did that pay for even a month of living expenses for the unemployed? Does that count as a bailout?

Have you felt that the government has helped you? Have you felt that the banks and corporate America have helped you?

They keep busy. They keep thinking up ways to get money out of your pocket. The government says it puts regulations on big businesses to help save you a buck, but they also are good at getting that buck back from you.

We were given this list from a reader. This is what the government does with its free time, it creates taxes. Here is a partial list of taxes.

- ✔ Accounts Receivable Tax
- ✔ Building Permit Tax
- ✔ CDL License Tax
- ✔ Cigarette Tax
- ✔ Corporate Income Tax
- ✔ Dog License Tax
- ✔ Federal Income Tax—Federal Unemployment Tax (FUTA)
- ✔ Fishing License Tax
- ✔ Food License Tax
- ✔ Fuel Permit Tax
- ✔ Gasoline Tax
- ✔ Hunting License Tax
- ✔ Inheritance Tax
- ✔ Inventory Tax
- ✔ IRS Interest Charges (tax on top of tax)
- ✔ IRS Penalties (tax on top of tax)
- ✔ Liquor Tax
- ✔ Luxury Tax
- ✔ Marriage License Tax
- ✔ Medicare Tax
- ✔ Property Tax
- ✔ Real Estate Tax
- ✔ Service Charge Taxes
- ✔ Social Security Tax
- ✔ Road Usage Tax (Truckers)
- ✔ Sales Taxes
- ✔ Recreational Vehicle Tax
- ✔ School Tax
- ✔ State Income Tax

✔ State Unemployment Tax (SUTA)
✔ Telephone Federal Excise Tax
✔ Telephone Federal Universal Service Fee Tax
✔ Telephone Federal, State and Local Surcharge Tax
✔ Telephone Minimum Usage Surcharge Tax
✔ Telephone Recurring and Non-recurring Charges Tax
✔ Telephone State and Local Tax
✔ Telephone Usage Charge Tax
✔ Utility Tax
✔ Vehicle License Registration Tax
✔ Vehicle Sales Tax
✔ Watercraft Registration Tax
✔ Well Permit Tax
✔ Workers Compensation Tax

Give them time and maybe they will come up with a Book Reading Tax.

These taxes were not part of our structure a hundred years ago. Back then, America was prosperous and indeed the most prosperous nation in the world. Now it seems that some of our politicians' ways are not prosperous at all, but quite preposterous instead.

Back then, we also had no national debt. NO national debt.

A lot of zeroes

Know what our national debt is now? It's over $17 TRILLION. That would be written with a one and a seven followed by TWELVE ZEROES.

You can Google "US National Debt Clock" and watch the number grow. It is $17,196,067,707,688 and some change right now, but will be different by the time this book gets in your hands.

It goes up $3.8 BILLION every day. We have been going billions deeper into debt every day since 2007.

I read that if every person in the United States kicked in over $50,000, we could pay off that debt. Why would we do that?! Did we incur that debt?!

Our "trusted" leaders did that to us. Let them pay it off.

Trust

The big boys in Washington and in corporate America say "trust me." Why in the world would we trust them now? What have they done to indicate any sign of trust?

They take our money and screw things up.

Not much to trust there.

You go to work every day and work long, hard hours to provide for your family. That is, if you have a job. The Congressman, bankers, and credit industry executives go to work too, they go to work to scheme. They cook up new ways to pilfer from your pocket.

Your Congressman works approximately 130 to 180 days per year. Do the math. 365 days a year. If we are generous and say that they worked 180 days, that is almost HALF the year. Those work days include campaign parties and stumping for election, too. What do they do with the other half of the year while you are working hard to support your family?

The corporate top dogs may spend more time at the office than the politicians do and they also spend a lot of work time on the golf course. They also spend a lot of time wining and dining those "hard working" politicians, too. Their work hours may clock in a bit higher than the boys on Capitol Hill, but the sweat on their brow only shows up when they're playing poker. A day's pay for a day's labor is meaningless to them. They do not know the meaning of toil or labor or hard work or scrimping to pay for groceries.

Your dollars

Every dollar you make has a purpose. Your take home pay needs to go for groceries, and gas, and the house payment or the rent, and the utilities, and school expenses, and doctors, and dentists, and shoes for the kids.

And, the credit card bills. Do you have credit debt? Yep, you are not alone. Most people have credit card bills. Because how else are you going to pay for it all? Some months are tight and the credit card is a way to keep afloat. Credit cards are a normal way to pay expenses these days.

> Credit cards are a normal way to pay expenses these days.

When I wrote the first *Debt Cures* book, our country's consumer debt was 2.4 trillion dollars. That is just a fraction of what the government has outstanding, but we as a people have a lot of debt, too. As of September 2013, consumer debt was over $3.0 trillion. That number does not include home mortgage debt.

Credit card debt then was $1.5 trillion of that. It has gone down to less than a trillion now. Latest stats for 2013 show a low of about $846 billion. That decline is not from people paying off their credit cards. It is because people have been defaulting on their credit cards.

So, don't for a second think that you are the only one with credit card debt. The average person had $8,000 in credit card debt at the first writing of *Debt Cures*, and now the figure is over $15,000.

Using credit cards is normal. Most people have credit cards and most people have credit card debt. There is no crime in using your credit card. The real crime comes in when the balance you have on that card multiplies out of control because of the tactics of the credit card companies.

We listed earlier some of the ways that the government sits around and thinks up ways to tax us. The banks and credit card companies sit around and think up ways to create more fees and penalties. They are out to get your money, any way they can.

Suits and sharks

The credit card executives may wear tailored suits and follow certain society manners and protocol, but they remind me of old fashioned loan sharks and "guys from the neighborhood" who enforced the payback.

The credit card creeps of today cannot charge usury interest, but it sure seems that way. Usury simply means charging an exorbitant rate of interest, and that is how it was in the days of thugs; now it is illegal. I still think the credit card company tactics scream of thugs and loan sharks.

Here's how it worked: You needed money and you were put in touch with Big Al. He would give you a loan for $1,000 and then charge you say 5% every week. Big Al and his goons would come by and collect 5% of that $1,000 every week. You would fork over a fifty, but you still always owed that original $1,000 loan. You never got to pay it off. They just keep coming by for the interest every week.

So, in reality, you'd be paying that loan forever. The original loan amount could never get paid down. You'd pay huge dollars over the life of the loan. In theory, you could end up paying $100,000 in interest on a $1,000 loan, and never be able to pay the original loan back. That's usury interest. That's now against the law. The thugs could go to prison.

Sounds appealing for the credit card industry of today, yes? You pay and pay and pay, and yet still have the original amount still sitting there staring at you. All you have been doing is paying interest and fees and penalties.

Rates

Do you even know what your interest rate is on all your credit cards?

Years ago, every state had a cap on what interest rate could be charged legally. In Massachusetts, for example, it was 21.74 %. If the bank or a credit card company charged you over 21.74% in interest, they could go to jail for usury interest, for exceeding the cap.

Well, the lending institutions do have a limit on the interest rate that they can charge today, so they can't technically get away with usury interest, but rates can get pretty high and the credit card companies are also great at nickel and dime-ing you. They have ways around the laws and regulations. And, how they do it actually is way more than nickels and dimes. Dollars and dollars.

Fees are big dollars and big business.

The name of the game in the credit industry is that dreaded four-lettered word. FEES. They have mastered the art of creating fees. These guys are creative and clever—and sneaky—when it comes to charging fees because "fees" are now the bread and butter of the credit card industry.

As long as they don't call the fees "interest," they are able to skirt around the rules. They make up a bunch of other names, they call it all some kind of "fee," therefore, it is legal. Late fees. Over the limit fees. Monthly statement maintenance fees.

Fees=profits

Fees are the profit center for this industry. The industry gets carried away, gets abusive in their practices and then regulations come along. They have to revise how they handle one area of fees. The taxpayer appears to be getting some relief. However, the banks and credit card companies are using their manpower to devise the next way to circumvent the regulations and create new ways to sneak fees in the back door.

They will get you one way or another.

For years, it has been an out of whack system. The feds are the ones regulating the industry. The feds also work with the banking and credit industry to create the laws and regulations.

Does that serve the American taxpayers?

Who is the robber?

If a robber broke into your home and stole your television, and computer, and jewelry and cash, would the government work with him to devise his regulations and penalties?

Let's set the scenario.

> Government: "Okay, Robber, you took the computer, television, jewelry and cash. We need some regulations here. You can only take the television and the computer. The jewelry and the cash have to stay in the house."

Robber: "Darn. Okay."

Government: "We will set up regulations that you must follow."

Robber: "Okay, I leave the jewelry and the cash."

Government: "That's right. No more stealing jewelry and cash. We'll be watching you now."

Robber: "Okay, pleasure working with you." The Robber now decides for himself to take the artwork, the electronics, and the meat in the freezer to make up for what he is not getting by taking the jewelry and the cash.

This scene may sound a bit outlandish, but the bankers and the credit card companies were given fair warning about what they could no longer charge in fees and they had plenty of time to devise new fees to charge. When the new rules kicked in that they had to follow, they were launching new fees to get that same money and even more into their coffers.

What did you get?

You pay your taxes every year to the government, and what do you get? Do you get to have real conversations about what you like, what you don't like and what is unfair? Of course not. You get senators and representatives who make deals with the industry lobbyists instead of working for you. That is just plain wrong.

But do you think they care? The politicians just want to get reelected and the bankers and the corporate dudes just want to keep making money. They want profits. They care about one thing, their own bank account.

They spend their creative energy devising ways to sneak money out of your pocket with new fees instead of devising ways to help you or ways to create better services. Maybe if they provided better service, they would make more money. Now there's an original thought. What do you think?

We all know situations when money is tight and the credit card came into play. For example, your car broke down. Credit card was needed to pay for the repairs. And, when it came time to pay the monthly bills the next month, things were still tight. You could not pay the credit card balance off in full and you mailed your payment in a couple days late. That's a normal real life scene.

> What started as a small balance has now grown by leaps and bounds...

The credit card company pounces. They loved to charge a late fee. The average going rate is $39. And, because you were late, they can increase the interest rate. Now you have a higher balance due to the car repairs and the monthly payment is higher and then they jack up the interest rate, too.

They love to kick a man when he's down.

Frustration continues

It's frustrating and downright maddening. I hear stories all the time. I bet you have one of your own.

We all know how it goes. You are in a pinch and you use the credit card. Life gets in the way and you miss a payment or you are late, and the fees start. And, the interest rate goes up. What started as a small balance has now grown by leaps and bounds overnight, and when the billing cycle comes around next time, you have a hard time paying it off. The debt starts to take on a life of its own. It can grow into something unmanageable and you have not even charged anything more on that account. It is nuts. It's crazy how out of whack the system is.

Did you know that the credit card companies can change your billing date at any time, too? You may be used to having your bill due on the 15th of each month and then it changes to the 13th. They like to catch you off-guard. They like to collect fees.

Imagine the balance due on your credit card is $1,000. Think how much fees and interest pile up on that. Imagine the balance due is $10,000. When you think of how much the fees and interest magnify that, it is the stuff financial nightmares are made of. The average person has $15,000 in credit card debt. That's a lot of interest and fees.

Do you catch any breaks? Do you get to take out the Congressman or the credit card creep and talk about it over wine and cigars? Do you get to make the rules?

Nope.

We can be outraged, and we should be. The tactics of the credit industry are downright offensive.

Instead of complaining, we can take their offensive tactics and throw it back in their face. The best defense is a good offense.

Game on.

CHAPTER 4

Don't Stay Stuck

"To err is human; to stick it to them and kick them when they're down is the credit industry way."
—Kevin Trudeau

The state of our country, and the world, has practically bottomed out, and yet, they still keep sticking it to us. People get their interest rates jacked up sky high with no warning and no explanation. A rate of 24.99% is common these days. One error on your part, making a late payment or not making the full monthly minimum and they get you. They charge a fee (or two or however many they choose) AND they raise your interest rate.

Take a look at all your credit card statements. Do you even know what rates you are being charged now? Do you know your due dates?

A typical story

We often tell the outrageous story of a guy who paid his credit card bill online on the due date. Repeat: He paid his bill on the due date using online payment.

He was charged a late fee. How can that be? The folks at Bank of America said it came in after 3:30 pm and any payments received after 3:30 pm are credited the next day.

They dinged him with the late fee AND for paying late, they DOUBLED his interest rate! This poor guy got hit upside the head twice. His rate was jacked up to 28.99%. The kind folks at Bank of America said if he paid on time for the next six months, then and only then, could he ask for his rate to be lowered. No guarantee that they would do anything about it, but don't even ask for six months. "We got you, sucker!" is what they seem to have said.

These instant rate hikes are unreasonable to say the least. Highway robbery is more like it. Just like the old days of stage coach and train robbers, these villains get away with it.

There was no bailout program for all the folks with credit card debt, but the credit card issuers got them. That's a head scratcher. Citibank took a $20 billion bailout from the government. Bank of America took a $45 billion bailout from the government. And, you know what Bank of America did a couple years later to say thanks? They let go of 30,000 American workers and hired overseas. Ain't that America?

A word like loyalty got lost in the shuffle somewhere.

Fine print

The Citigroup execs don't blink an eye when asked about their policies. They maintain that everything is right there in the fine print. Ah, the dreaded fine print. If a cardholder does not want the rate increase, they can opt out, but they must close out their account. It's their version of saying: It's our way or the highway.

The Fine Print is that little twenty page brochure you get with a credit card offer. It is tiny font, with no spacing. They don't want it to be easy to read. It is legalese that few can read or understand. It is designed that way so you glance at it, and throw your hands up in frustration. How many people actually read that stuff?

The boys in Washington keep spouting regulations and watching the industry. They talk about changes being made to protect the consumer. Nice talk.

Remember when Christopher Dodd, the Democrat from Connecticut, was the Chairman of the Senate Banking Committee? He proclaimed that he wrote "tough" legislation, but it never passed. Look at the records. Millions upon millions were donated to his campaign from the financial industry. When CNN asked about that connection, his office did not respond. However, his office did make the point that they tried repeatedly to pass credit card reform regulations and were met with "stiff opposition from the credit card industry."

> It is legalese that few can read or understand.

Give me a break.

Backstage may have sounded like this: "I try to tell the fellas that they have to go along with my regulations and reforms. They say no and they give money to my campaign. Gee, what's a guy to do?"

Know what Senator Dodd did after retirement in 2010? Took over as head of the Motion Picture Association of America. Maybe his acting skills were put to good use there.

Feeling secure?

The current Chairman of the Senate Banking Committee is currently Tim Johnson. He, too, is good at rhetoric. The current state of the world banks is anything but secure. The financial crisis of 2008 is still looming over our heads. How many years will it linger?

The troubled economy still seems to be pretty troubled. Banks are not getting kinder and gentler.

You want to open a new checking account? That requires a higher balance these days.

You want to use your debit card in a foreign country while you're on vacation? That is going to cost you a higher fee now.

You want to use an ATM that is not part of your bank? That is going to cost you three bucks at least.

Fees. Fees. Fees.

Some banks used to offer customers free overdraft protection by doing a balance transfer from a savings account or equity line. Now they ding you a fee every time. Many banks are following suit. Common customer courtesies have gone the way of the agreement by a handshake—they do not exist anymore.

The fees on overdrafts alone topped $32 BILLION for 2012 fiscal year.

We pay more and we get less.

Fee frenzy

Any fee. Any time. Need to stop payment on a check? It will cost you more. Want a cashier's check? It will cost you more. How about using your own debit card at your own bank and getting cash from it? It can cost you a fee.

Have you been hit with a fee lately? Overdraft? Was it thirty bucks? $39? More? Ninety percent of bank fee income comes from overdraft and non-sufficient fund (NSF) charges.

What are banks in business for? These days, it's to collect fees.

You don't have to stay chained to your current bank. Besides using your mattress or a cookie jar, you can switch your money to credit unions or brokerage accounts or smaller community banks. You can get a check-writing account at your mutual fund place and usually with no fees for checks or ATM transactions. Shop around. There are online banks too now like Ally and PNC Virtual Wallet.

The traditional ways are changing. Look into other options. One cure is simply stop thinking you are stuck with your bank. You're not.

They lure you in

The banks and the credit card companies want you to think you are stuck. They want to keep you in their clutches.

The banks and credit card companies lure you in and entice you to use their cards. They tell you to charge, charge, charge. They want your monthly payments and your interest and your fees. They don't want you to pay off your balance. They want you in their money pit forever, paying a little and always their prisoner.

In an old *Business Week* report, one gal who went on record to confirm this. Cate Columbo states that she was a call center customer service representative at MBNA, which was bought out by Bank of America.

She said that her job was to "develop a rapport with credit card customers and encourage them to use more of their available credit." It was all a big game to Cate and her co-workers. She was good at her job and claims that her colleagues would gather around her as she bantered sweetly on the phone with a customer, chanting "Sell, sell." Cate lured the unsuspecting customers to their doom of never-ending payments.

> They want you to stay down, uninformed.

Now listen to what Cate said: "I knew they would probably be in debt for the rest of their lives."

The motives of the banks and credit card companies are to keep you paying them. You are their revenue source. They want you to stay down, uninformed. They don't want you to pay on time, they don't want you to read the fine print. And, they don't want you reading books like this that can change your way of doing business with them.

They are not looking out for your best interest. Have you realized that by now? The one to look out for you is YOU. You are smart. You are ready to learn what it takes to get out of debt and not be their dummy.

You've learned a few tricks already. Make at least the monthly minimum payment to avoid a fee. Pay at least a day ahead if paying online and send at least a week ahead if you are using check via snail mail. There is no need to let them be able to change you a fee and thus give them the "right" to jack up your interest rate.

If you don't like your bank, switch.

It really can be that simple.

CHAPTER 5

The Rules

"The credit card industry plays by its own rules."
—"Secret History of The Credit Card,"
PBS Documentary

It is outrageous and ridiculous what the lenders and banks and corporations keep getting away with. It is still mind blowing that the US government allows them to make their money by screwing the American citizen.

Banks and lenders and credit card companies are taking advantage of people every day.

The guys in the suits don't care if you file bankruptcy. They don't care if you lose your house. They don't care that you are in debt up to your eyeballs and are being hounded by collection pit bulls and you can't sleep because you lay awake worrying. Point blank, they just don't care at all about you.

Don't fool yourself. They don't give a rip about you or your circumstance. The banks and the credit institutions and the credit card companies and the mortgage companies and all the consumer lending companies, and the President and the boys and gals in Washington, they really don't care.

I had a banker tell me once, "We are given a license to steal from the American citizen." A license to steal! Signed, sealed and delivered compliments of Uncle Sam and our United States government. That's why we're having such a credit crisis today—because these banks were handed a free pass to filch from the American public.

Look where it has got us!

Do you feel you have been served? Do you feel you have been listened to? Do you feel you have been cared about?

NO!

Money grubbers

They are the most self-serving industry, the money grubbers. They took advantage of millions and we ended up with a recession beyond belief. Foreclosures. Bankruptcy. Unemployment. Horrible housing market. Gloom and doom.

And, it still pervades.

Their profits are the motivator. Not customer service. Do you have $30 billion in profits? I didn't think so.

$30,000,000,000

The credit card industry of FEES is a $30 billion-plus industry. The industry executives making those ludicrous profits have forgotten what it's like to live in the real world. The $30 billion in credit card profits is coming from you, the hard-working American citizen who uses the credit card to pay for the necessary stuff of life, not the latest designer duds or Hollywood plastic surgeries or trendy vacations.

Credit cards are what get us through the crunch times. And, then they—the credit card companies and the lending institutions—come along and kick us when we're down. And, the federal government looks the other way.

We have had enough.

Game on. Are you ready? Are you ready to fight back for yourself, and all the people who have lost their homes? Are you ready to fight back for the people who have lost their jobs? Are you ready to fight back for the people who are underwater in their mortgages?

When you fight back for you, you are fighting back for ALL.

Let's do this!

American Dream

The American dream is that of a resilient people. We are strong and we are smart. We don't have to keep taking their garbage.

We have learned that trusting them is not the answer.

Who can you trust? YOU.

You simply need to know what to do and how to do it.

That's what *Debt Cures - New & Updated* is all about. Giving you the game plan and strategy to overcome the big boys.

A great starting place is knowing all about your credit report and your credit score. We'll cover that so you can play your best game. Credit reports and credit scores are the backbone of the credit lending business, so it is imperative that you know what they are looking at—how they are judging you. They are judging you, don't you forget it.

They don't play fair. They judge you harshly and extremely critically. There is no such thing in their mind as giving someone the benefit of the doubt. The powers in charge want to find ways to make your credit score and credit report negative and damaging to you so that they can charge you higher interest rates and more fees.

> Credit reports and credit scores are the backbone of the credit lending business...

It has become really twisted. People with really good credit scores are no longer the ideal customer for the banks and credit card companies. It is so totally backwards! Someone with a great credit score who pays back their loans on time should be a banker's dream. But no, think about it.

The banker and the credit card company want people who will pay, yes, but will take a long time to do so. They want the middle of the pack. They want to know that they will get their money, but they want you to be a little late sometimes so you thus allow them to ding you with a fee. When you are late or miss a payment or do not make the monthly minimum payment, that opens the door for them to go hog wild with fees and to jack up your interest rate.

That is where they salivate.

The "good" customer

The good customer who pays on time and in full every month does not get them the best bang for their credit dollar. A PBS special reported that the bankers call these "good clients" deadbeat. That's how messed up the credit world has become.

These folks are scheming and tactical.

What do they live for?

Interest!

Fees!

Penalties! Monthly payments that keep trickling in forever.

We'll cover the best strategies for credit scores so you can stick it to them and get the best deal for you.

A separate world

If you read the first *Debt Cures* book, you may recall some stories from the show called The Secret History of Credit Cards. Anyway, in The Secret History of Credit Cards, a Harvard law professor, Elizabeth Warren, stated that nobody else would be able to run a business like the credit card industry is allowed. She pointed out that the credit card contracts are written in such a way that is unheard of in any other type of industry.

They are an entity unto themselves. They operate in their own orbit, twirling around with their pals in Washington.

Professor Warren used the example of buying a big screen television. The customer signs a contract to pay the $1,200 for the TV, with a normal amount of interest for the privilege of paying over time. That's standard, normal.

The credit card companies don't do that. That same television can cost oodles more because they can keep jacking up your interest rate. They can end up doubling, tripling, or even quadrupling that amount and they can get away with it!

No one would ever sign a contract that said: "This TV is worth $1,200, but I will pay you whatever you change your mind to every month and I will keep paying forever." With interest and fees, that is what can happen.

It is no exaggeration that people have made a single purchase and their credit card balance has grown exponentially due to interest and fees.

The credit card and consumer loan industry is unique because they can get away with this unbelievable behavior. Can you think of anyone else who operates with these tactics?

Imagine you hire a painter to paint your house. He charges you $2,000 for the job. You agree and sign the contract to pay $2,000. When the job is done, he bills you for $2,000. If you do not pay in full the next month, he cannot come back at you and say, "Now the job costs $4,000. Pay up."

That is not how the business world works.

If you were to not pay him, he could take you to court, but he cannot just keep upping the amount that you owe. "Oh, look, another month has passed. Now that paint job costs you $6,000."

A private industry

The credit card companies exist in their own little world, where they can do almost anything because they have highly paid lobbyists wining and dining the Congressman in Washington. Have you noticed that the laws and regulations stay in the favor of the credit lending industry?

You can turn the tide.

First off, you need to realize that you can get yourself out of debt. Be advised that you do not need to pay a service professional to help you. You just made a needed investment and it's this very book. Hopefully, you also signed up for the monthly *Debt Cures* newsletter. Obviously, we can't put out an updated book every month, but the newsletters are terrific at keeping you aware of the credit card industry and its latest shenanigans, and what you can do.

You really do have the power. You do not need to pay a credit repair person to make phone calls for you. YOU can do that. I tell you how. You do not need to pay someone to consolidate your debts and create one payment. YOU can do much better than that. I tell you how to ELIMINATE debt, not just roll it all together. Any of the "fixes" that those kind of agencies do for you, you can do for yourself. Believe it. Simply knowing that you do not have to pay big bucks is a step toward curing debt and creating wealth. The more money you keep in your pocket now, the better off you will be.

You DO NOT have to hire a credit repair firm. You DO NOT have to hire a debt consolidation agency. You DO NOT have to live in a state of depression or panic. YOU have more power than you realize.

The banks and the credit card companies want to keep you in bondage to them. They want you as their monthly slave, shackled to fees, and interest, and penalties. They do not want you to know that you hold the key to your own freedom. You can unlock those shackles and walk away.

The key? It's all right here.

If you have already filed bankruptcy, don't despair. There are instances when that is the most feasible option. Many a millionaire has come from bankruptcy. If you are simply feeling overwhelmed, don't despair. Bankruptcy does not necessarily have to be the solution. Keep reading and you will discover ways to cure your debt.

No matter what your situation, there are many ways to cure your debt and build your wealth. There is so much you can do. Are you ready?

CHAPTER 6

Credit Score Basics

"What you don't know about credit can hurt your personal finances on many levels."
—Laura Adams, *Huffington Post*

What you don't know can hurt you. The more you know, the more you realize that you do not have to take the garbage that the credit card creeps keep rolling out.

Do you know your credit score? Have you looked at your credit report? When I wrote the first *Debt Cures* book, I quoted a statistic from a 2003 survey that said over 90% of Americans had no idea what their credit score was. Thanks to the millions of copies sold of my book, that stat has to have changed. Millions more of you now know your credit score and the importance of the credit score and what it means to you.

Your credit score matters because the better the score, the better interest rate you can get. Remember how we discussed earlier in Chapter 5 that folks with good credit scores are no longer a banker's dream? In the good old days, a lender would love you if you were a good credit risk. They give you money and you pay it back with a little interest on top. Everybody's happy. It was a win-win.

Now they want the guy who has good enough credit that they know they will get paid back, but they also want to jack up the interest rate. It's like they secretly whisper, "Sure, we'll give you a loan or a credit card, but you are gonna pay!"

If you know your credit score and stay on top of your credit report to ensure the best score possible, you will get the best rate possible. The lender might not like it, but we don't give a hoot about what he wants. He will be looking for any way to be able to raise your rate. It is your duty to look out for yourself. The lenders sure aren't going to. They want those interest bucks!

Credit matters

Think about it. On a $200,000 mortgage, just one percentage point can make a difference of $45,000 in interest! Having a good credit score can save you thousands. Depending on your situation, a great credit score can even save you a million bucks.

During the course of your life, getting a better interest rate and better terms on every transaction all adds up. Better you pocket that money than the lender!

Your credit report is really important. When is the last time you looked at yours?

In the first *Debt Cures* book, a lot of pages were devoted to the nitty gritty basics of credit reports. If you need a refresher or are new to credit reports, we give the condensed version here. It is just as important as ever, so I also give updates in the monthly *Debt Cures* newsletter when new information or action occurs affecting credit reports and credit scores.

Not every single transaction you make gets reported on your credit report, but a lot does. Your financial patterns are being monitored and your financial history is being tracked. The theory behind the whole credit report concept is one of fairness. In the good old days, the bankers and credit lenders knew their customers and loans were passed out with a signature and a handshake. Society grew and the folks in charge of lending out the money no longer knew everyone. A system had to be devised to determine who should get a loan. A score seemed to make sense. A credit score was invented to be a barometer for creditworthiness. If each person were judged independently and objectively, any creditor could thus make a determination on any individual.

The credit report is supposed to be just that, objective and fair. Every person's transactions with creditors are reported and a report is generated. It shows who you pay, how much you pay and when you pay. Every month, your bank, your mortgage company, and your credit card companies send in the data on you. In theory, it sounds like no big deal. It sounds like it is "fair."

The reality is a bit different.

How it works

There are entities that collect this financial information on you, called credit bureaus or credit reporting agencies. The primary three are called Equifax, TransUnion, and Experian.

Every month, what you pay on your loans and credit cards is reported by the credit agency or lender to any of the three credit reporting agencies. They crank the numbers into a formula and something is spit out called the credit score.

Well, actually, they don't do the number cranking. That is handled by another company, a software company called Fair Isaacs

Corporation. The score that they compute is called the FICO score because it comes from this company.

> ...calculations are geared to produce the lowest number possible...

The FICO score is the main score that is used by mortgage lenders, loan agencies, and credit card companies. The exact formula for the FICO score is a closely guarded secret, like the identity of Deep Throat. But that secret came out. The details of how the FICO score is calculated is shrouded in privacy. Which is stupid, really.

They create a score to "fairly" compare all borrowers and yet they don't reveal what the score is comprised of exactly. You are being graded, but you don't get to know the details. The secrecy is because they don't want you to know how they manipulate the numbers to work against you. The algorithms and calculations are geared to produce the lowest number possible, not the highest.

What they want

High credit scores mean good for you, bad for the lender. Not so much a game based in fairness, is it?

The credit authorities do not want glowing credit scores. They want to be able to hit you up with bad interest rates and fees for the "privilege" of letting them loan you some money at killer terms. The mathematical engineering done to the reported data is a mystery, yet credit experts have done enough research to teach us some important tips.

In general, the credit score is comprised of five parts. Your payment history, your current amounts owed, the different types of loans you have, how long you have had credit, and your new credit accounts.

The exact details are not known of how the computations work, but the general consensus is that the overall score is totaled up and weighted by 35% Payment History, 30% Amounts Owed, 15% Length of Credit History, 10% New Credit, and 10% Types of Credit Used.

About.com gives a simple explanation of what the credit score formula is comprised of:

✔ **35%—Payment History**

Takes into consideration the number of accounts you have; if you have any collections activities or negative public records, like judgments, lawsuits, or bankruptcies; if you have any delinquent accounts: total number of past due items; how long past due; how long since you made a late payment.

✔ **30%—Amounts You Owe**

Takes into the computation how much you owe on your accounts and the types of accounts you have with balances; how much of your credit lines you've used; the amounts you still owe vs. the original balances; the number of zero balance accounts.

✔ **15%—Length of Your Credit History**

This is the total length of time tracked by your credit report; the length of time since your credit accounts were opened; the time that's passed since the last activity. The longer you show good credit history, the better your score.

✔ **10%—Types of Credit Used**

This takes into consideration the total number of accounts you have and the types of accounts (credit cards, mortgage, car, etc.). A mixture of accounts usually generates better scores than having a bunch of different credit cards. It is such an irony—they practically throw credit cards at us, yet the credit score goes down if you have too many credit cards.

✔ **10%—New Credit**

This is the number of accounts you recently opened; the proportion of new accounts to total accounts; the number of recent credit inquiries; the time that has passed since recent inquiries or newly-opened accounts; if you've re-established a positive credit history after encountering payment problems.

The credit reporting agencies turn in information on you every month and every month, your score is updated. Every month, they are looking for ways to bring you down. I read a report that the formula is based on ways to lower the score and that there are eighty-eight points to knock you down a notch.

How is that for fair?

Not that fair

Eighty-eight ways to bring down that score. I have no idea what they all are, but every time you make a late payment, it gets factored in. If you miss a payment altogether one month, another whammy. If you have too many credit cards, that is a black mark against you. The system created for "fairness" is not fair at all.

It is what it is. They use it against you. You can use it for you. The credit report and the credit score are what lenders look at when you apply for a loan or a credit card. Thus, it is important for you to get your credit report, know your FICO score, and learn how to improve it.

Because nothing is clear cut or simple in the world of credit reports and credit scores, you need to get all three of your credit reports. Get your credit report from each of the three credit bureaus, Experian, TransUnion, and Equifax

Why all three? Because they are each slightly different. Why? Not every creditor reports to all three. Why? I have no idea. The system is a bit ridiculous.

You want to look at all three. You want to see what your creditors see about you. And, you want to make sure what has been reported about you is correct.

Chances are there could be some errors. Reports state that 90% of all credit reports have errors.

Review your report

You need to go over yours with a fine tooth comb to make sure each is an accurate reflection of your credit history and habits. You want the best report/score possible. Every point you go up in credit score is potentially many, many dollars saved in interest.

Over the life of your loans, many dollars are at stake.

You are entitled to get a free copy of your credit report every year. You can request each report separately from each agency.

Equifax
P.O. Box 740241
Atlanta, GA 30374
1-800-685-1111
www.equifax.com

TransUnion
P.O. Box 2000
Chester, PA 19022-2000
1-800-916-8800
www.transunion.com

Experian
P.O. Box 2104
Allen, TX 75013
1-888-397-3742
www.experian.com

You can also use the service at www.annualcreditreport.com to get all three at once. The form to use is available online at ftc.gov/credit and www.annualcreditreport.com.

If you don't have internet access, contact them by mail or phone.

Annual Credit Report Request Service
P.O. Box 105281
Atlanta, GA 30348-5281
(877) 322-8228
www.annualcreditreport.com

There is also another player in the game. Another web site called CreditKarma.com also offers free credit reports. Note that there are many sites online that offer credit reports, but many ding you with a fee or charge you a monthly subscription or some other gimmick.

Be wary when you are surfing the internet. Only use sites you know and trust. That applies to everything, not just credit report web sites.

Credit Karma's starting point is to give you your free credit report. It really is free. They do not take your credit card information to charge you like many of the others.

Our researchers pulled this from the Credit Karma web site: "When you access the free credit score, Credit Karma will show personalized offers to you based on your credit profile. These offers are from advertisers who share our vision of consumer empowerment. If you wish to take advantage of Karma Offers, it is up to you. Credit Karma will never share your information without your consent."

Take charge of your report and your life

Make sense? You can get your credit report for free and after that, you get to choose what offers you want. Based on your credit score, the partners who affiliate with them will make offers to you. That is how this site is able to give you a free report, because they are getting paid by advertisers. You don't have to pay and you don't have to accept offers either.

Some internet companies do the bait-and-switch method and you think you are getting something for free, when you really got tricked into something.

> ... take time to really review all the line items.

You can get one free copy per year at each credit reporting agency and at Annual Credit Report. You can also now check in each month to monitor your score at sites like www.creditkarma.com, too. Bottom line—however you do it, do it. Get your credit report.

When you get your reports, take time to really review all the line items. Make sure that even the basic information is yours.

If that sounds fundamental, it is. You probably are not the only person in this country with your name, so it is very possible that incorrect information could be on your report. Make sure all the accounts listed on the report are really yours.

This is important.

Mistakes happen

Credit reporting agencies make errors all the time. The lenders turning in the information make mistakes, too. It is worth your time to review to ensure everything on the report is your account, your name, and linked to your Social Security Number.

We also live in a world of identity theft. That's the other reason to review your credit report frequently. There could be stuff going on in your credit report that is not yours, because somehow a hacker got your information.

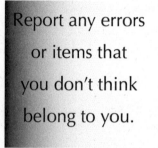

Report any errors or items that you don't think belong to you.

It is extremely wise to be vigilant about identity theft. Monitor your credit reports to be sure that nothing is there that is not yours. If you see any suspicious activity going on or accounts that you have no knowledge of, report it right away.

Identity theft is all too common and does not seem to be getting better. The fraudsters are getting smarter and smarter. That means you need to be smart with your private information. Do everything you can to keep your financial data to yourself.

Spend some time going over your reports to make sure that your credit report is accurate. Report any errors or items that you don't think belong to you. You report directly to the agency who issued the report. You can also contact the creditor to get the ball rolling there, too.

The credit reporting agency has thirty days to respond to your dispute of an item. If they cannot resolve the issue, they must remove that item from the credit report.

Dispute

If you have anything fishy, get it off your report. This can have a huge impact on your credit score.

Especially if you are applying for a loan, you need to see the credit report first. You need to know if there are trouble spots that need to be taken care of. Claim your dispute and get those questionable items off your report. That is the time to apply for a loan. When you know your credit is in the best standing you can reflect.

FICO credit scores range from 300 to 850. Arbitrary score, arbitrary numbers. It is what it is, so we work with it.

Current attitude is that anything under 580 is not good. You won't get a good interest rate or terms. A score from 580 to 680 is "average." From 680 to 700 is "good." If you have a score in the 700 to 850 range, that credit score is considered "very good."

There are some sites on the internet proclaiming what the average FICO score is and yet FICO does not release that information. They like to be secretive. Some say that the average American credit score is 682. Some say 692. Both of those scores are considered good.

One blogger states that the median FICO score as reported by FICO several years ago (and since then they have said nothing) is 723. That would be very good.

What do you say? Do you feel the average American has a good credit score and is getting good rates? What about your personal score? Where do you fall? Was a lender willing to work with you?

Credit scores may always be a source of mystery, but we know plenty. There are concrete ways to raise your score and get a better deal when you apply for a loan or credit application.

The internet is loaded with "professional services" out there trying to get you to pay them to help you boost your score. Not necessary. Do you really think you need to pay someone to help you raise your score? Isn't that why you bought this book?

You can do it yourself. Starting right now.

CHAPTER 7

Improve Your Credit Score

"'Fixing' a credit score is more about fixing errors in your credit history."

—myfico.com

Even the folks at FICO know that errors abound. They also know that what you see may not be what you get.

The Consumer Financial Protection Bureau (CFPB) released a 2012 study comparing credit scores sold to creditors and those sold to the consumers. The study found that about one out of five consumers would likely receive a meaningfully different score than what the lender gets on them.

The numbers don't match up.

You apply for your credit score to see what the mortgage company or banker or credit card company sees about you and your finances and your payment history and all that you have been doing since you entered the financial world. You get a report, so you think you know where you stand with the guy giving you a loan.

Now it comes to light that the report the creditor gets is different than what is reported to you. What gives?

The press release from the Consumer Financial Protection Bureau (CFPB) stated: "This study highlights the complexities consumers face in the credit scoring market," said CFPB Director Richard Cordray. "When consumers buy a credit score, they should be aware that a lender may be using a very different score in making a credit decision."

The complete report is called the "Analysis of Differences between Consumer and Creditor-Purchased Credit Scores:" and is available at: http://files.consumerfinance.gov/f/201209_Analysis_Differences_Consumer_Credit.pdf

Protection for consumers

Look at the name of the CFPB. Consumer Protection. This Bureau had to be created because the financial industry was taking advantage of the consumer, using abusive and deceptive practices.

> ...the financial industry was taking advantage of the consumer...

This bureau was created as part of the Dodd–Frank Wall Street Reform and Consumer Protection Act. This act, named after Barney Frank and Chris Dodd, the fat cats at the forefront (what senator doesn't love the spotlight?), was passed in 2010. Barney Frank was the House of Representative's Financial Services Committee Chairman and Christopher Dodd was Senate Banking Committee Chairman.

The Act's purpose: "An Act to promote the financial stability of the United States by improving accountability and transparency in the financial system, to end "too big to fail", to protect the American taxpayer by ending bailouts, to protect consumers from abusive financial services practices, and for other purposes."

The Wall Street Reform and Consumer Protection Act came about as a response to the hard-hitting recession and made, supposedly, big changes to the financial industry's way of doing things. There had not been this broad of an act by the government since the aftermath of the Great Depression.

What does that tell you?

This "recession" that the government continued to try to downplay was actually a pretty big hurt. Duh.

Rules

The Act had over 200 new "rules" and as we can see, the big boys keep creating new rules to outstep whatever regulations get put on them. The lenders should have rules and adhered to them, and then perhaps we could have averted the financial crisis that occurred.

If the mortgage folks would not have gone crazy with subprime mortgage loans, where would this country be right now? A whole helluva lot better off than it is right now.

There's a little thing called trust, and the very act that the government has to pass an "Act" and create a consumer protection bureau tells you where things stand.

Right now, the issue of the credit report is at hand. You get one to look at, your creditors get another one to judge you. So much for taking care of the consumer there. Now that the CFPB is aware, time will tell what new rules and regulations get passed along.

The wheels turn slow in Washington.

For now, the Bureau recommends that consumers consider the following advice when they get or want to get a credit score:

"Shop around for credit. Consumers benefit by shopping for credit. Regardless of the scores different lenders use, they may offer different loan terms because they operate different risk models or face different competitive pressures.

Shop it

Consumers should not rule out seeking lower priced credit because of assumptions they make about their credit score. While some consumers are reluctant to shop for credit out of fear that they will harm their credit score, that negative impact may be overblown. Inquiries generally do not result in a large reduction in a consumer credit score.

Check the credit report for accuracy and dispute errors. Credit scores are calculated based on information in a consumer's credit file. Inaccurate information may be the difference between a consumer being approved or denied a loan. Before shopping for major credit items, the Bureau recommends that consumers review their credit files for inaccuracies. Each of the nationwide credit bureaus is required by law to provide credit reports for free to consumers who request them once every 12 months."

The Bureau began supervising consumer reporting agencies as of September 30, 2012. That's a big hell yes. The CFPB's supervisory authority will cover approximately thirty companies.

The Bureau's examiners will be looking to verify that consumer reporting companies are complying with federal consumer financial law, including that the companies are using and providing accurate information, handling consumer disputes, making disclosures available, and preventing fraud and identity theft.

What that means is that when you file a dispute with the credit reporting agency, now someone is looking over their shoulder, and their paperwork, to make sure something is done about it.

It's a start

It means a point for you, the average American consumer. Score one for the little guy. A day late and a dollar short, but a hollow victory is a victory and a start. The act is, of course, many days late and many dollars short. Years of foreclosures and millions of homes lost.

The mortgage crisis that swept our nation was beyond belief and beyond explanation. Thousands and thousands of innocent people lost their homes, their dreams, because they trusted what the bankers and the mortgage lenders and the federal government told them. It did not seem improper for these folks to trust those so-called authorities at the time. A lot of the mortgages were the result of a government initiative. "Let's let everyone experience the American dream," they boasted.

Too bad for all those people now who have no home of their own. The enticement was too great. "Sure, you can buy a house." "Of course, you can afford that monthly payment." "All your paperwork is fine."

Lies. Greed.

The CFPB didn't exist then.

The mortgage companies gave out mortgages during that crazy time that they would never have taken on when they were doing business by legitimate business standards. Many of the people had shaky credit scores and the ability to repay was based only on the first year of the mortgage. These folks were not good credit risks.

The lenders didn't care. They were taking in short term and not thinking long term ramifications.

Look where it got us.

Out of hand

The credit industry game of wanting the customer to pay late so they can charge a late penalty fee got a little out of hand. Late payments become the norm because these borrowers were in completely over their heads. It became an explosive nightmare. These folks were not properly informed because the ones in charge who should have informed them were not doing their jobs.

The only true Consumer Financial Protection Bureau is you.

The late payments and the defaults turned into a big rolling snowball. It took everybody out.

A lot of people, uniformed, unprotected people, got burned. It started the avalanche of foreclosures. It led to the housing market collapse. Unemployment reared its ugly head as the economy tanked. Things went from bad to worse to worse.

How are you now? Still trying to rebuild your life? Don't let yourself get caught in their web of lies. Even with a watchdog government agency now trying to maintain order, you still have to look out for yourself.

The only true Consumer Financial Protection Bureau is you.

When you are shopping for a home loan, know the real situation and run the numbers yourself. Know what you can actually afford. Don't let anyone talk you into something because on paper it "looks good."

Because of the fallout, the pendulum went the opposite direction and the lenders stopped giving out credit. They went from lazy, lousy, anything goes to nothing gives or goes. They shut up shop and didn't give out loans.

That didn't help either.

Once an idiot, always an idiot,,,

The banking and lending industry is calming down and the purse strings are open again. Loans are being made to qualified buyers.

So how do you know if you are a qualified buyer? That's when the credit report comes in. You need to know the score.

Whether you are shopping for a home mortgage, a car loan, a student loan, a personal loan, a credit card, whatever the credit matter, you need to know how the lenders size you up. All they care about is your credit score, so the first order of business, no matter what your situation, is to get the credit score up as high as you can.

If you have a good score, it won't matter so much if you get a different report score than the one they pull on you. You will have a good score and be able to fight for your rights. To protect yourself and your money, get the best credit score you can.

FICO

Get the actual FICO score, not the scores on the various reports. The credit bureaus give a ballpark figure, but mortgage companies usually only look at the real FICO score. The different credit reporting bureaus generate their own scores now, too, just for kicks and confusion. You may request a score thinking it is the FICO score and it's not. You could get something called the PLUS score or the Advantage Score.

What do you want? The FICO score.

It costs a fee, even for the credit agencies, to get the FICO score. It's just a few bucks. You can get yours through www.myfico.com.

Then get down to the real business of this book, improving your credit score. Get out your credit reports and play along at home. Some of these fixes are instant. Some could take 30 days. In the big picture of life and how much money a good credit score can save you (thousands and thousands), thirty days is nothing and definitely worth it.

Get the free copy (copies) of your credit report.

✔ Fix any easy errors:

✔ Name, Date of Birth, Social Security Number, etc. Correct it.

✔ An account that is not yours—have the credit reporting agency remove it.

✔ An account that was closed and is showing as active, have them correct it.

✔ An account that is showing as closed and is still active, have them correct it.

These quick and easy fixes can make a quick and easy increase in the score. (All you have to do is contact the credit bureau and show your documentation; it's a very painless procedure.)

You want an accurate representation of what is really your story. Make it read the best you possibly can.

Review the payment history. If you are getting hit for a late payment and you paid on time, you need to file a dispute.

Any kind of error like this, dispute it. You will recall that the majority of your credit score is based on these kinds of payment detail items.

Send in your documentation with your dispute. You can file the dispute online very quickly and then follow up with your paperwork via snail mail. The credit reporting agency has thirty days to verify your claim and resolve your dispute.

If they cannot do so within thirty days, they must remove the questioned item from your credit report. Removal of a negative item has a huge positive impact on the credit score.

File disputes. Here is a helpful hint from some friends who are real estate experts and all millionaires: File disputes. In fact, I would call that advice magic.

I talk about Magic Words, and that phrase could count.

If you want to get a loan and your credit report/credit score is less than stellar, you can beat the industry players at their own game.

Timing is everything. If you are under the gun to get a loan, filing a dispute means that the questioned items have to be removed (after the 30 day window). Until the credit reporting agency can prove that, in fact, the item must remain on your credit report, the questionable negative items are removed from your status.

Your credit score, when these items are removed, will be amazingly improved. That is the credit score that the lenders will see and use to determine your rate and loan terms. You can get a tremendous boost to your score thanks to your genius and impeccable timing.

That one tip helps countless people. Magic Words. File disputes.

Monitor your credit reports. You can use a credit monitoring service to do this, sure, or you can rotate getting your free copy from each credit bureau every few months. You can also use places like creditkarma.com. Any items that are fishy, question them. Get them off your report. Repeat. Get them off your report.

Delete. This is another one of those little known "secret" techniques that is a huge score booster. Chalk this up as a Magic Word too. Delete.

> Instead of showing the collection as "paid," they can delete it...

If you have an account that went to collection, call the collection agency. Simply ask if they will delete it from your record if you can pay.

Having a collection activity on your report is not good. Having it show paid is better, but not having it there at all is best!

This is highly possible. Instead of showing the collection as "paid," they can delete it from your record. Half of all collection agencies will do this.

Many of them do not require you to pay off the full balance. Pay a chunk of it (get the money however you can; have a bake sale, sell your Beanie Baby collection, whatever) and get this clunker off your credit report.

The benefit to your credit score is worth the hassle of coming up with some money to pay.

Deleting it means it does not get included in the scoring computation at all. At all. Understand?

Having it show as paid still means a black mark against you. Collection activity is one of the buggers that the formula looks for to ding your score. Remember, the score formula is rigged to have 88 points to penalize you. This is one of them.

Having a collection action gives a major wallop to the score. Getting it deleted is like a magic boost to the credit score. It makes an AMAZING difference. If you have a highlighter and are marking up this book, highlight this section. In this case, you want to remember the Magic Word DELETE.

There's 50 ways to leave a lover and just as many to leave your credit score hanging out there in the wind. Having a good credit score matters. You will get a better deal and interest terms on loans and credit applications.

Measuring stick

Did you also know that the folks lending you money are not the only ones who use the credit report as a tool to measure you?

Your employer and potential employers can have access to your credit rating. They can judge whether they want to hire you based on your credit history. Is that fair? Some say no. If you had a tough run and were late on some payments, why should that hinder your ability to get a job? It has nothing to do with your qualifications. You want to get a job to improve your situation so you don't get in that bind again.

Your insurance man also can take a peek at your credit report when determining your rates. A bad credit report can hurt you in many areas of life which is why it is important to have the best score possible.

A glowing credit report and you can shine in all areas of your life.

Re-read what has already been written in this chapter. Those pointers alone can jack up your score. There are more ways to boost that credit score, of course, some so obvious that you are probably shaking your head wondering why you never thought of it or why other people aren't teaching the same suggestions.

Make phone calls

Call all your credit card companies and ask if they will increase your credit limit. That's it. On this call, all you ask for is a credit increase. This is an easy call to make. They are not going to give you the run around.

You will get their attention. All you want is the ability to give them more of your money. That's how they see it. The higher the credit limit, the more you will charge. They will see visions of more interest and fees, and maybe even begin to salivate at the thought.

They do not need to know that you have no intention of spending more with the new credit limit. You want it so you can show that your balances are not using up all your available credit.

That's right. You simply want more wiggle room. You are judged on how much available credit you use. So get more available credit.

Your FICO score is primarily concerned (65% of it!) with your payment history and what you owe. 35% is payment history. 30% is amounts owed.

It seems like it should be so easy:

✔ Pay your bills.
✔ Pay on time.
✔ Pay enough on each.

It should be that simple, but it's not.

The powers that be in the FICO world don't want you to use all your available credit. If a credit card issuer gives you a card and a credit limit for $5,000 because you are a good credit risk, you should be able to use that $5,000.

However, if you do, the FICO gods will strike you down.

Using all your available credit is one of the 88 demons that will bring your score down. The FICO folks want you to use less than 30–35% of your available credit line. Stupid, stupid, stupid, but that is how it is.

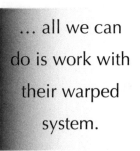

... all we can do is work with their warped system.

If anyone can tell me why that makes sense, please do so. Since we don't have a say-so in how they come up with the score, all we can do is work with their warped system. The quick, easy, no cost way to do this is to have the credit card companies up your limit. Therefore, your percentage of what you are using looks better to the FICO scorers.

Spread your balances

Another way to meet the silly requirement of not using all your available credit is to spread around how much you owe among all your cards.

Play the shell game. For example, say you have a credit card with a $5,000 credit limit. You have charges on that card totaling $4,000. You are using 80% of your credit line.

Seems all well and good, and it should be. However, the idiots in the FICO factory who manufacture your credit score think that is a reason to punish you.

So what you do is spread that balance around to your other credit cards. Take the $4,000 that you owe on this credit card and split the balance among your other cards.

Most credit cards have balance transfer options. Many give checks to use or you can call and talk to a customer service person to do the transaction over the phone. All you need is the credit card numbers and billing address of the cards to take on some of the balance due.

This card in question had a $5,000 credit limit and you had $4,000 on it. To stay within the FICO formula limits, you should have about 30% max charged on that card, $1,500. Spread the remaining $2,500 on to cards and run the math real quick to stay in the 30% range for those credit limits, too.

Also, pay attention to interest rates. Know what interest rate you will be paying before you make a balance transfer. Many cards allow intro rates of 0% for balance transfers, yet you still have to pay a fee, usually 4%.

You don't want to move a bulk of debt to a card with a high interest rate if you can't pay it off. Getting hit up with more interest charges defeats your purpose of playing their game. You are in it to get lower scores and lower payments. Don't shoot yourself in the foot by switching to a high interest rate card just to get a lower credit limit percentage.

Pay down your balances

Your credit card balances are the pawns here, and the credit industry wants to use them against you. Do whatever it takes to get those balances down.

Sell something. Get a second job. Borrow from a friend or family member at a really low interest rate. Whatever you can think of to come up with some cash to get those balances down to the 30% range.

Got old wedding rings? Sell them. Bikes you never ride? Sell them. Skip vacation this year and get those balances down. The less you owe, the less interest you are paying out as well. The less you owe, the better interest rate you get on everything, too.

When you are serious about cleaning up your credit report and credit score, sometimes you have to take drastic measures. That means paying attention to every dollar and where it goes. You think you are living free by spending willy-nilly. In fact, it's the opposite.

Careless spending costs you and you end up paying them way more than you realize. Is that what you want? To give your hard-earned money to the credit creeps?

Bust open the piggy bank, the change jar, and the money hiding in the mattress. Pay off your credit cards and you will be the richer and wiser one.

We teach you how to pay as little as possible and get those balances paid.

Savings

Take a long, hard look at your savings account. What's it earning you? What are you paying out in interest on your debt?

If you are carrying credit card debt and need to get those balances under control in order to get the credit score under control, think about your "savings" plan.

Maybe you have been trained to save. That's a good thing, don't get me wrong. More people should be trained how to save and to spend less. Our forefathers paid themselves first and then spent the rest on their needs. They didn't have credit cards to lure them into debt. It was easier to save then.

Some folks save now. (Stats show that not many do, however.) For example, let's imagine you have a payroll deduction every two weeks that goes into your savings account. An automatic savings plan is not a bad idea, and I'm not knocking it, but if you also have a large amount of debt hanging over your head, are you really saving anything?

> ...you have to cut savings and get credit debt taken care of.

What does a savings account pay these days? 4%? Doubt it! Maybe 1%. How much are you racking up each month on your little nest egg?

How much is on your credit card balances and do they have an interest rate of anything like your savings? Again, I doubt it. Most credit cards are around 15%.

The interest that you are earning on the savings is not keeping pace with the amount you owe on the debt. When there is debt to be paid down, you have to cut the savings and get the credit debt taken care of. When your balances are minimal, then jack up your savings plan again. You will see how the numbers shake out and how it makes sense.

Pay your bills on time

Some of the most basic strategies of money management cannot be overlooked. If you have credit card debt (and face it, who doesn't?), and you are working on improving your credit score, start at square one. Pay each month on time.

No rocket science there. But let's be honest, do you always pay your bills on time? We are all fallible human beings with jobs, kids, PTA, the mother-in-law coming to visit, the pain-in-the-butt boss, groceries to buy, laundry to do, a school science project due (tomorrow), a birthday gift to buy, and a hundred other things every day that take our attention away from the monotony of paying the bills.

Things slip through the cracks. It happens.

Even with the ability to pay bills online, late payments can still happen.

Now that you know how much a late payment affects your credit score, you will have renewed vigilance. You can set up bills to be automatically paid every month online or make a schedule to review bills each week if you write checks by hand.

Unforgiving

The credit people are very unforgiving in how they calculate the FICO score, and it is the truth that little things mean a lot. Little things that we can control, we should control.

Mailing your payment timely or setting it up online to be paid on time should now be a priority for everyone. Late payments are like dollars blowing out of your wallet and into someone else's. It's like burning a twenty dollar bill (or more) for every late payment. When you pay late, you are giving the creditor the right to hit you up with an outrageous late fee, and they then can also jack up your interest rate. Triple whammy and even worse, you set yourself up for the whammy of the bad credit score.

Never miss a payment

We just talked about being late and how damaging that is to your credit score. A missed payment is a killer too. No matter what, send in your payment, even if it is late.

Skipping a payment is bad, bad, really bad. One missed payment and they will use it against you. That is grounds to jack up your interest rate, too. Skipped payments are a killer for the credit score as well.

If you are going through tough times, ignoring your payments will not make the situation any better. After a couple of missed payments, creditors now are ready to turn your account over to collection. Not much grace exists these days.

Having collection agency activity on your credit report is one of the biggest score killers. It brings your credit score down like a lead balloon. It is one of those lingering items, too. It can hang around, weighing you down for up to seven years.

When you find yourself behind the eight ball and cannot make your payments, either on time or at all, call your creditors. Don't ignore it. Pick up the phone and negotiate some kind of payment arrangement. Any payment will reflect better on your credit than hiding under the bed wishing it all would just go away. And, it will go away eventually. Hang tight and you will learn methods to cure your debt.

Don't close old accounts

Sometimes people are surprised to learn that they should keep old accounts open. If they are not using that card, they assume they should close it and say goodbye. Not always.

One of the ways to improve your good credit score is to show that you have a history of good payment.

If you have a credit card account that you no longer use, but it shows that you always paid and always paid on time, then keep it open. If your old accounts were troublesome and your track record was not so great, go ahead and close them. Make sense?

Keep the good stuff on your record. There is no harm in having old accounts around if they are good. Use that card every once in a while to keep it active. Pay it off immediately when you do use it.

A good item on your credit history can counteract some of the other negative items. Credit experts say that the best thing for your credit score is to have accounts with good payment history of five years or more. It shows you are a good credit risk. If you have accounts like this, keep them open.

Don't have too many credit cards

Easier said than done in our credit crazy world. Every day you are bombarded with credit card offers. Ignore them. One or two cards are all you really need. How many do you have in your wallet? How many cards do you have that you don't carry with you?

> ... credit score calculation holds it against you if you have too many accounts.

Most people have more than two.

The credit industry has a double standard. The credit card issuers want you to get all these cards. They mail you offers every day and hound you at the mall and sporting events. It's easy sometimes to have lots of credit cards. They entice you to sign up with their great offers.

However, the credit score calculation holds it against you if you have too many accounts. Not fair, but what have we mentioned in this book that is fair?

A word to the wise, department store charge accounts are usually not worth it. They charge notoriously high interest rates and have high fees if you make a late payment. The little bit of savings they give you with the initial offer (usually 15% of your purchases that day) do not warrant opening another credit account.

Don't have too many loans

Same with having too many credit cards, having too many loans in general is not considered a plus in the credit score calculation.

You might be a credit magnet and able to get credit easily. That should be a good thing. However, if you have too much credit going on in your life, the FICO formula folks seem to think that is bad.

You are a good credit risk so lots of people would give you money, but the calculation is devised to have that be a black mark against you. Crazy, I know.

Even thinking about getting a loan or credit can affect your score. Every time you apply for credit, be it a credit card or a car loan or a personal loan, that creditor requests your credit report to check you out. Every time someone requests your credit report, it is logged into the system as an inquiry.

Too many inquiries are deemed negative.

Another stupid example of their warped methods. If you have good credit and want to take out a loan or get a credit card, for whatever reason, who really should give a damn how many people have inquired into your credit.

If you have good credit, you have good credit. But the system is rigged against you and too many inquiries will drag down your credit score.

While you are doing the work of raising your credit score, do not apply for any new loans or credit card offers. Clean up the credit score and make it work to your advantage.

An FYI: You requesting your own credit score does NOT count against you. Also when a a credit card company does a preliminary check on your credit report before sending you a pre-approved credit offer in the mail, that does NOT count against you. You certainly have no control over that. Those inquiries are called soft inquires and are not counted against you.

Pay more than the minimum payment

If all you do is make the monthly minimum payment as stated on your credit card bill, you will be in the hole taking their garbage forever.

Credit is a way of life, no doubt about it. It's easy. Many people these days never carry cash. A debit card or a credit card is accepted anywhere these days, and now in some places, a mobile app payment. That is handy and convenient and also makes it easy to spend. So, one way to cure debt is to avoid the splurges and the impulse purchases.

That said, I want to repeat that I realize most of you are not in debt because of your "reckless spending." The credit card companies want to paint the picture that they are faultless and the people are to blame for the debt in this country. We know that is not true.

Some people put everything on their credit card in order to get miles or bonus points or some kind of reward. That is fine if you can pay it off each month. The reality is that most people cannot pay their balances in full each month.

The balance keeps getting bigger every month.

The credit card bills grow because of a job situation or a medical issue or a divorce or a death or a move or school or…

The credit card bills also grow because of fees, fees, fees, fees, fees, fees, and interest and fees.

Pay wisely

To escape their credit creep clutches, their nonstop fees and interest, you have to make more than the minimum payment. If all you send in is the bare minimum, you are in their clutches forever. A $3,000 balance could take nearly 20 years to pay if all you pay is the minimum monthly payment.

> If all you send in is the bare minimum, you are in their clutches forever.

The required minimum payment is different depending on the issuer of the card. It is 2-4% of your total balance. Think that through. You only have to pay 4%. Sounds good when you are in a pinch. But that means 96% of your balance sits there unpaid. Month, after month, after month.

What is the interest rate on your account? How much are you dishing out each month in interest? How much of your principal balance is actually getting paid on?

You will never get ahead if you continue to stay stuck in minimum payment mode. They are not being "nice" by letting you pay such a low amount; they are laughing all the way to the bank.

Say you have a balance on your MasterCard of $1,000. You only have to make a payment of $40 ($1,000 x 4%). Don't fall into their greedy trap. With an interest rate is 14.9%, you do the math. You get dinged more in interest fees than the monthly payment. How will you ever get ahead? How will you ever pay this $1,000 balance in full?

If the credit card companies have their way, you won't. Customers for life is what they want, and not because of your loyalty and their great customer service.

You can keep sending that little check every month and never make any headway or get anywhere close to paying it off.

How do we stop the game? Easy. Make more than the minimum payment. Say you wanted to have this account paid off in a year. Instead of making the monthly payment suggested on the billing statement (you don't have to listen to their suggestions), you know that you could afford to pay $100 every month.

If there were no interest, then obviously this debt would be wiped out in ten months. Even with the interest, by paying $100 each month, you can have this bill gone in a year's time. If you went along with the suggested minimum payment, it would take over two years and at least twice the interest.

Calculate it

You can find online calculators to estimate the monthly minimum payment and how long it will take to pay off your balance. That was one of the changes that came with the new regulations. Credit card companies are now required to post this on your statement. Take a look to see how long it would take you to pay off your balances if all you paid was the monthly minimum.

The banks and the mortgage companies and the lending institutions and the credit card companies do not want you to know everything I just told you in this chapter. What you don't know does hurt you. They like to keep it that way.

As you can see, what we just covered here is not brain surgery. It's not anything monumental. All it takes is you getting your report and taking some action.

Your credit score is just a number and if the credit industry wants to make it a numbers game, we can too.

If you apply these simple little tricks and techniques, your credit score can go up higher and higher. That means they will not be able to punish you with a high interest rate. That means you get better payments. That means you get less interest, less life of loan to pay on, less hassles and headaches.

It better be obvious by now why you should pay attention to your credit score. It simply equates to more money. Who do you want to get that money—you or them?

Measure up

For years now, and no change is on the horizon, the credit score is the measuring stick of the consumer credit industry. They want you to come up short. You know now how you can measure up.

It's up to you, but in my opinion, if you want to give your money away, give it to your favorite charity; don't give it to these clowns and greedy bastards.

Why does it matter? The best way to illustrate the differences in the impact of the credit score is using an example of three friends who all want to obtain a mortgage loan.

For example, to keep it easy, they each want a $500,000 mortgage and are buying similar homes in the same town. Get it? They all want the same kind of deal.

The difference in the deal they get is based upon their credit scores.

The difference in credit score means a different outlay of cash for the same thing. Do you want to be stuck paying thousands more for the exact same thing as your neighbor? Same floor plan, same neighborhood. You end up paying more simply because you have a lower credit score. That's motivation to improve your score!

A Stooge Story

Moe, Larry, and Curly all get their credit reports and credit scores. Moe has a score of 700. Larry has a score of 675. Curly has a score of 620. They go together to the Big Bank to apply for a 30-year fixed mortgage.

These scores are not too extreme, yet the difference does matter. A few points of FICO goes a long way. The higher the score, the better the deal.

The bank looks at the credit reports and gives them all 30-year fixed rate loans. The interest rates are different, based on their scores.

Moe gets a rate of 6.25%. Larry gets a rate of 7.0% and Curly's interest rate is 7.5%. These rates are not typical for the market now as we still are experiencing record low interest rates, but it shows the point dramatically how this much difference in interest rate creates different money going out the door. It's only a percentage point, right? So it seems like it shouldn't make that much difference.

It does.

First off, compare monthly payments:

Moe	$3,078
Larry	$3,326
Curly	$3,496

Curly will have to fork out $418 more each month than Moe. That adds up. Multiply that by twelve months and he has dished out an extra five grand.

The interest rate you get is based on your credit report. What you pay out is based on your credit report. It is very obvious why the credit report matters when you see the numbers, especially over the 30-year life of the loan.

After thirty years, this is what each paid out in interest:

Moe	$608,290
Larry	$697,545
Curly	$758,586

That's a lot of money.

After thirty years, Curly paid over $61,000 more to the bank than Larry and a whopping $150,296 more in interest than Moe.

$150,000.

Credit score matters now, doesn't it?

Taking the simple steps to improve your credit score means THOUSANDS of dollars in your piggy bank and not some banker's yacht.

It's YOUR money. What do you want to do with it?

CHAPTER 8

More Credit Score Secrets

*"Federal law guarantees consumers the right to
dispute and remove credit report errors."*
—CreditCards.com

The world of credit scores keeps getting more crowded and more confusing. Pop up ads appear as you as surfing the internet telling you how to get your free credit report and many of those sites are not actually free. You also get bombarded with ads on how to instantly raise your credit score and those folks usually want your money, too. It's easy to get lost in the maze of "must do this" and "must not do that."

With the economy still in the toilet, folks are still disgruntled about their financial situation and want ways to get ahead. That's understandable. Just be smart and be cautious before you throw money at quick-fix ideas. You can get the info you need to better your situation by reading books like this.

Even with the advent of other credit scores, the system that is still the big dog is the FICO score. Most mortgage lenders use the

FICO score and most of the largest lenders in the country for all other loans and credit cards still rely on the FICO score.

Secrets

The inner complexities of the scoring process are a closely guarded secret, and the exact formula is never disclosed. That in itself is not fair. If you have to take a test, you should be told what is expected of you. Not knowing the grading process is ridiculous.

The whole credit world is quite ridiculous.

The folks at Fair Isaac and the credit bureaus want to keep you in the dark. It is just one indicator that the credit industry is skewed in favor of the creditors. No surprise there.

> It is just one indicator that the credit industry is skewed in favor of the creditors.

And yet, even they can't play nice with each other. Back in 2008, there was infighting and lawsuits among Fair Isaac and the big three credit reporting agencies (Experian, TransUnion, and Equifax) when the FICO score formula was going to be revamped.

With the crash of the economy, they wanted the score process to better predict who will default. Perhaps the bankers and lenders should only give loans to those who are able to repay, that could be a nice starting point. Some common sense and some standards would go a long way. The bozos in the suits started the whole mess and the cleanup seems to continue on forever. The fallout still has not truly subsided.

We keep sludging on through the mess.

The details of the credit score formula and any tweaking are not known ever, however, the scoring emphasis is still as follows.

Need to know

Credit limits—Now more than ever, the scoring process puts the screws to you if you are using too much of your available credit. Unfair, yes. But no one ever said Fair Isaac was fair.

Your score can drop several points simply because you are too high on your credit limits. Using your available credit is going to hurt you. Now with the crash of the economy, creditors were also stiffening the available credit limits they give out. They were also cutting credit limits on existing accounts, so take note of what your limits are and what your balances are.

And, now the creditors are slashing your credit limits willy nilly.

As we talked about earlier, do not run up your balances too high on any one account. Spread your balances out over all your existing accounts and pay down whatever you can, however you can.

Active accounts—This is another stupid thought process on the credit scoring formula. You can get points deducted from your FICO score due to few "open and active" accounts.

It is damned if you do, damned if you don't. They want you to have open and active accounts, but don't you dare carry too high of balances anywhere.

On one hand, they persecute if you have too many inquiries into your credit and then on the other hand, they cut your score if you do not have many good open accounts. What the hell do they want?!

When the recession was in full swing, some creditors were closing down accounts. They pulled the rug out from under you causing your score to get penalized through no fault of your own.

The strategy is to maintain open, active, and not delinquent accounts. Have several good accounts, pay on them (every month and on time, of course) and as stated above, do not run them up to the max of their credit limits. Got all that?

Collections—this one is good news. This change in the weight of the scoring process is one for the little guy. Small collections issues—meaning the original debt is under $100—are no longer looked at by the scoring spiders. The old score system would give a negative ding for any kind of collection activity. The small chump change stuff is now off their radar. No big deal, but any way to avoid a point against you is a good thing.

Authorized users—The original plan of the updated version of the FICO formula was to ignore any authorized user data in determining the credit score. They wanted to do so because of the scammers who were selling "authorized user" availability to folks wanting to get instant good credit. It was a way for credit repair companies to help their clients get better credit. It was, however, not that person's credit. So the FICO folks wanted to take away the whole thing.

Think how unfair this is for many, many people who are legit authorized users of a loved one's account. There are countless spouses who are the authorized user on a joint credit card and have no real credit in their own name. Take your own mother or grandmother, for example. Maybe she never worked outside the home. The man was the breadwinner. The woman ran the household and did everything else. She, however, had no real credit history of her own.

Spouses and children have long been authorized users in order to start a credit rating of their own. They could piggyback on the good credit of a parent or spouse. The abuse of others almost caused the whole thing to be tossed out. The lenders, of course, wanted this feature to be scrapped because they don't want anyone to get a boost in their credit score. But in a last minute cave, and probably because legal experts warned that ignoring information regarding spouses on authorized credit lines could be a violation of the Equal Credit Opportunity Act, FICO agreed to allow authorized users to stay part of the credit scoring process.

Inquiries—Originally, in the revamp of the formula, inquiries into your credit history were going to have less of an impact on the score. Seriously, applying for credit is not a predictor of default. That is the reason they stated for taking another look at the scoring process.

As it shakes out, nothing really changed, so you still need to be careful about how many inquiries into your account are happening. If you are shopping for a loan, do not go around opening credit applications.

The bottom line is that the lenders and the folks in the FICO world want to run the world. They can manipulate things to their advantage and as long as they can, they will.

Protect your score

Protect your credit score by doing all the things we discussed earlier. The less of your credit lines that you use, the better. Even if you pay every month, running up the balance is bad for your FICO score.

The score does not distinguish between balances you pay off and balances that you carry from month to month. Seems stupid, I agree, but you gotta know what rules they are playing with, so you can play along.

If you use one card for business travel, for example, and run the balance high each month, stop doing that. Use no more than 30% of the available credit limit at all times. The best thing for your score is to use less than 10% of the credit on that card. On all cards.

I know, it is not fair and it does not make sense. But we know it, so we just have to deal with it. Ask for a higher credit limit on the card that you like to use for travel or use several cards so none shows a big balance at any time.

If your creditor limited your available credit and you have a large balance on that account, do something about it. Call them up. Ask to get back your original credit limit. Most people don't pay attention to what is going on and most people don't know that they can pick up the phone and ask for a higher credit limit.

Also, do what you can to pay down the balance so you are at less than 30% of your total available credit. Transfer part of the balance to another card with more available credit. Now, more than ever, the credit score rates you on credit limit. Play the game now that you know the rules.

The credit score secret: It is better to have small balances on many cards than a large balance on one card.

Don't close old accounts

In our initial explanation of credit reports and credit scores, the point was made to keep accounts open and active. May we emphasize it again: Keep your accounts open. Do NOT close out old accounts if they were in good standing. You get more points in your credit score for having open accounts in good standing. You get hurt for having a higher proportion of closed accounts.

The FICO system wants several accounts in use and in good standing. Give it what it wants.

A good way to maintain this habit is to put a small, regular monthly charge on each card and have automatic payments set up. You want to keep it active each month and you want to always remember to pay each month. The trick is active and in good standing.

> By making payments on time every month, you jack up your credit score.

Credit cards are considered "revolving" accounts. Car loans and mortgages are installment accounts. They have a set fixed payment every month. Your credit score likes to see you have both kinds of accounts.

You don't have to run out and buy a car or a house. You can get a small installment loan, a small personal loan. By making the payments on time every month, you jack up your credit score. And, getting a loan can be a way that you pay down those other credit balances, too. Keep an open mind. And, yes, keep an open and active credit account.

Credit is key

Knowing about the credit score process and how they use it and how they compute it puts the power in your corner. We live in a world where credit scores are key. You want the key to turn in your favor, to unlock doors for you.

As the world keeps spinning, the FICO folks add their spin, too. A recent CNN report also explained that what you get to see as your credit report may not be exactly what the lender is looking at. That said, you do everything in your power to have a good score, no matter what. Make sense?

If your history is good, they can't hurt you. Plain and simple.

This CNN report stated that the FICO folks compute scores flavored for anything a lender may want. They reported there are 49 possible FICO scores a lender may receive. That's more than 31 flavors of ice cream. How we need that many permutations is a mystery.

You receive your one blanket FICO score. The lenders have a menu to choose from depending on what kind of loan you are applying for. If you are applying for a car loan, the lender can get an auto loan FICO score on you. If you are applying for a credit card, the issuer can get a special bankcard score on you.

There is, of course, a FICO mortgage score. There's also an installment loan score and a personal finance score that specifically focuses on your history of using financing companies—for example, if you've signed up for store-branded credit cards.

CNN states: "Even though newer versions of FICO's scoring software are being used, many credit reporting agencies continue to make older versions of the software available to lenders—adding to the overall number of FICO scores for each consumer."

That explains why there can be 49 different FICO scores floating around out there. The exact details of each are not released to the public, but the gist has been explained here. If you play by these rules and do regular checks of your credit report, you can maintain a healthy FICO score, regardless of what version of the formula they are using to evaluate you.

The lenders want to hone in on a specific area of your credit pattern. You get the general FICO score reported to you. The experts say that the difference in what you see and what they see is perhaps 15 to 20 points different. It could actually be in your favor, too.

If you did well on all car loans, and that is what the lender is looking at, your late payment on your JCPenney card might fall under the radar.

Scoring models

The discrepancy in scores is now under the watchdog eyes of the Consumer Financial Protection Bureau. They will look at the different scoring models and what the three credit reporting agencies are doing and compare the scores between those three and what the consumers see.

Beside the FICO scores, and all its various mutations, other credit scores are out there, too, like proprietary scores developed by the credit bureaus themselves (like PLUS and Advantage scores), and scores you can get from private companies like Quizzle.com, CreditSesame.com and CreditKarma.com.

It's enough to make your head spin.

"The grand total number of credit scores is truly countless—so while 49 FICO scores seems like a large number, it's really a drop in the bucket," said John Ulzheimer, a former FICO manager and now at smartcredit.com. "The good news is that proper credit management transcends all credit risk scores. If you do the right things, you'll have a good score across the board.

Got that?

Do the right things and screw them. Your best attack is to have a good credit score. Then they can't hurt you.

Stellar credit

The tight-lipped folks at FICO remain so, but some information does get leaked.

About one-fourth of the consumers in the FICO data base have what is considered good or stellar credit scores. The common things they did put them in the top tier. You, too, can be a gold star credit report holder. Do what they do.

To be in the range of 785 or higher, you have to have debt. There is no credit score if no one is giving you loans. You have to be active and have debt. That is how you pay it off and show how great you are.

> You have to be active and have debt. That is how they judge you.

Some people think the opposite. If they never have a loan, they think it shows how good they are with money. Maybe, but for a credit report, you have to be using credit. That is how they judge you. Folks with good scores have debt. The average top score person has four accounts that are active and in use. These people also have an average of $8,500 in debt.

Here's an interesting note. We know that the max to use on your accounts in just 30% of your credit limit. An analysis of the high scoring folks did much better than that. They used just seven percent of their credit lines.

That means you have to have a lot of accounts to tap from, if you have big balances. Share the love with all your accounts.

Age matters

It pays to age. The older you get, the better your score gets. (In general, of course.) Longevity does matter though. Credit history, as in having history with a creditor, boosts your credit score. The folks in the upper tier of credit scores had old accounts. Over ten years is good. Some even had accounts that had been ongoing for 25 years. That shows your reliability and the FICO factor eats that up.

The secret to high scores is no secret. FICO loves folks that pay on time. 96% of top dog scorers never miss a payment. Did you know that missed payment can stay on your record for seven years? Seven years it can haunt you. That is why you always make a payment. One time of being forgetful can affect you, so get in the habit of remembering.

If you get turned down for a loan, the lender has to give you a copy of the credit score that was used to judge you. This came in the Dodd-Frank act and although it sounds nice, really, what good does it do you to get your score after they have rejected you?

If you use your cards to rack up points and still pay them off each month, your credit report may still get dinged. It depends on the timing. If they pull your report, they may see a lot of balance there, not the payoff the next month.

Unfair? Yep.

However, if you have a high balance account sitting there, paying it down can have an immediate boost to your score. It's a game and usually it's rigged against you.

If you have balances at the end of the billing cycle, that is what gets reported. That is what affects your credit card. The billing cycle shows a big balance at the end of every month, even if you pay it off the next month. Make sense? Try paying it off before the bill comes due and see if anything happens to your score.

Use a card one month and pay it before the billing cycle ends. If all they are doing is looking at balances, see if you can wrangle it to where at month end, you have no balance. It's tricky, of course, because month end, or cycle end, or whatever, is arbitrarily based on what the scorers decide to look at.

Many of folks have tried this tactic though and it works. Pay in the middle of the month and your score can go up.

Credit tactics

Another successful tactic used by some is to accept all the credit card offers that come your way in a given amount of time. The initial round of those inquiries into your history will give a temporary ding, so do not do this if you are applying for any kind of loan. After about six months, having all that available credit will help your score.

The key is to use each card once in a while to show activity and that you are using your credit. That is how you are judged—by how you use the credit, not just how much you have. Don't run up the balances. Some folks do not do well with lots of cards with lots of credit sitting there tempting them. It is a strategic move to better your financial situation by upping your available credit. Don't blow up by upping your debt. This is about you keeping your money and not giving any more to them.

This is a great primer on how to improve and maintain your credit score. Not too tough. Just do it.

Don't forget the strategy to dispute items, too. Especially if you are applying for a loan, you want to get that heavy weight item off your report, even if just temporarily. Many people don't know how to dispute an item, and no surprise here either, the review of the dispute on the other end is pretty shoddy sometimes.

Under the Fair Credit Reporting Act, credit reporting agencies are required to thoroughly investigate your credit report dispute. Even if you know the lender made the mistake and you contact them to fix it, you also need to file your dispute with the credit reporting agencies. This is how you keep yourself covered.

You can take it up with the lender, too, but if they don't come through, you cannot sue them unless you have filed the dispute through the proper channels, which means reporting it to the credit bureaus.

Track your records

Keep track of your records and when you send in your dispute. If you get no response to repeated dispute claims, you can file a claim with the Consumer Financial Protection Bureau. If you get frustrated, you can file suit against the credit reporting agency, but make sure to file a claim with the CFPB first. You want to cover all your bases.

You've got to show evidence that you have been financially harmed by their not fixing the mistake on your credit report. Keep all records of what you send them and when you send it. Have the postal confirmation receipts that they did indeed receive your paperwork. Keep copies of all rejections you get based upon your credit report and you can show how that could have been avoided if they would have corrected your report.

The credit bureaus have ways you can file disputes online. Don't do it. File in paper via snail mail and keep copies of everything. Doing it online is hasty and does not give room for you to fully show your case.

It is better to give them too much than too little. They can deny your dispute if you don't provide enough information and documentation. Give it to them.

Send the lender exactly what you send to the credit agency, too. You are disputing with both. You need to show this in case it does not get resolved. If you go to court, you need to show that you did everything in your power to give them accurate information. This is one area to not be lazy in.

There is plenty of information out there online about credit scores. Every month, in the *Debt Cures* newsletter I provide breaking news as it happens and helpful information on how to play the game to beat them.

By applying the techniques, you can absolutely improve your credit score. Seriously, you can change your credit score and you can change your life.

That is what I love with these books. People write in and say, "Kevin, the information you gave me changed my life." You could be one of those people. Are you ready?

CHAPTER 9

Combat Collection Creeps

"The Better Business Bureau and most state attorneys general report that consumer fraud, which includes debt collection and other types of scams, consistently ranks among the top 10 complaints."
—Wall Street Journal

Consumer fraud ranks among the top ten complaints. Ain't that America?

One former debt collector is now breaking her silence. Marissa N. states: "I used threats and intimidation any way possible. I was trained to do that. One way or another, I'm going to get you to pay me."

Threats. Intimidation. Talk about taking school yard bullying to a new level. One man who was being hounded by debt collectors said he felt like it was the mafia coming after him for his debt.

Old "mafia" debt collector Marissa says, "There are techniques that can stop debt collectors' calls. I just don't feel the people know about them."

She's right. People don't know about them.

Until now.

Teach the children well

Financial education needs to be available now and offered to everyone. Kids are not taught this stuff in schools. Most parents are not educating their kids on the ins and outs of how to handle money. Our kids need to learn how to handle their money because it is pretty obvious that the government and the banks and the credit card companies don't want them to know anything.

They want us all to stay in the dark so they can keep sucking their money out of pockets and wallets and bank accounts.

It would be nice if the schools could teach some basic facts about money and debt and credit cards. Since our public schools are government funded, money matters will not be high on the priority list for graduation requirements.

Ya think?

Therefore, it is up to us to school our children, and each other. Call me biased, but I think the *Debt Cures* books should be mandatory reading for every young person before they head off to college. Would you like me to gift wrap them as graduation gifts?

Kids today, no, everyone today, needs to understand that the credit industry does not give a rip about the consumer. It is up to us to protect ourselves.

Credit worlds

The credit world consists of two sections. One section is the people that loan you the money. The folks that issue credit like the credit card companies, the banks, the mortgage companies, the payday loan companies.

They make outrageous money by charging all these outrageous fees. Their mission is to get what they can out of you and bury you in debt.

They do what they can while they have you in their clutches to bleed you dry. They also know that they are not going to be able to collect on everyone. It's a numbers game and odds are that some people will not be able to pay.

So, the other section of the credit world, the other evil villain, is the collection agencies. Stories like Batman—and the financial world—have more than one villain.

> ...one more way to make money off you—they sell your debt to an agency...

The credit companies don't care that you are suffocated from debt and can't pay them. They suck you dry and then they pass you on to the next level, their cohorts in creepy tactics, the collection thugs.

The lenders are not all that upset about it. It is just one more way to make money off you—they sell your debt to an agency or they hire a thug to be their goon.

Now, we have a whole host of collection agencies willing to buy all these debts. It's a thriving industry, too. Debt has not suffered a recession.

Collection story

Let me give you an example. Let's say that you owe $20,000 on your credit cards and can't pay it off. Pretty ordinary.

In this scenario, I'll play the role of the collection agency. I cut a deal with your creditor. I buy that balance that you owe them for pennies on the dollar, maybe for as low as $1,000.

So now, I own that debt. The original creditor took their baby grand from me and called it a day. As for me, the Collection Agency Bulldog, I paid $1,000 for a $20,000 potential pay day. I like my odds.

Why? 'Cuz I will try like hell to get you to pay me whatever I can. The $1,000 I paid out is an investment. The creditor just made a grand by selling it to me. He says goodbye and good luck. Whatever I can get out of you is all mine.

I now stand to make $20,000, if I can get you to pay. I crack my knuckles and laugh with crazy man glee.

See how it works? The bank or the lender or the creditor gets something and writes off the rest. Now the collection guys have a chance to get more out of you, too.

The Evil Collection Agency Owners are pretty much pond scum. Their tactics are known throughout the land to be less than proper. They will stop at nothing to get money, so be ready and be warned. Consumer fraud is a top complaint, remember? These are the guys creating those complaints.

They hire telemarketing guys, an outbound sales crew...schemers, liars, scoundrels. These are ruthless individuals who will call you and hound you to death. They're paid on commission and they are the most competitive breed of animal on the planet. These vermin will say anything to make a buck.

Remember that the thug only paid $1,000 for the pleasure of harassing you. Anything he collects over a $1,000 out of you is pure profit. So, if he gets $10,000 or $3,000 or $2,000 or whatever, he doesn't care. He will be out celebrating his victory and laughing about how bold he was to get it.

Intimidation

Those collection creeps make my skin crawl. They use their mastery of lies and intimidation skills. They will do whatever they can to get money out of you and in their pockets. They call it chump change because they see you as the chump.

But are you a chump? No way!

The collection agents are trained to lie. They're trained to deceive you. They're trained to harass you. In many cases, what they're doing is against both federal and/or state laws. But many people in this country don't know that. They fall prey to the bullying and the threats, and they send them money.

Don't do it!

These guys don't expect to get the whole twenty grand. They know that if you had it, you would have paid the first creditor and not be in collections. They know that they scare the hell out of you though and make you cough up something.

Resist. Don't fall for it.

Their fear tactics are just that.

People are afraid when they don't know what to do. I will tell you what to do so you don't have to shake in your boots if you get a call from a collection thug.

Wise up

First of all, the number one reason to not pay the collection harasser is that YOU MAY NOT OWE THAT DEBT.

I repeat: They often scare people into paying a debt that is not even their own. That's how good these guys are at their jobs.

Don't fall for it. Why in the world would you want to pay something you don't have any responsibility for?! Holy crap, no!

It does not matter if the collection guy is a guy who bought your debt or is a collection thug hired by the creditor who did not sell your debt and is trying to put the squeeze on you, you simply need to know what to do.

Rule #1. Do not panic.

Repeat rule number one when the creeps call. They want to scare you. They want to intimidate you. They want you to think they have power over you.

This is how a typical collection call goes:

The collection thug calls you and launches into a tirade. He makes all kinds of claims and accusations. They call repeatedly and at all hours. They know stuff about you. They get under your skin. They will say anything to unnerve you.

It may go something like: "I have record of your debt to ABC Company in the amount of $10,000 and I demand payment of $1,000 immediately. If you do not send payment immediately, I will seize your house, I will seize your car, I will garnish your wages at your job, I will seize your children, I will seize your child support, I will seize your alimony, I will seize your iPhone, I will seize your television, I will take away your life."

Okay, this may be over the top, but that is what they do. They launch into stuff to scare you.

They want you to shut them up by saying you will send in a payment. Don't do it. Do not send one red cent.

They will usually ask for a payment, not the whole balance. They want to get your goat. Or something like that.

Rule #1 again, do not panic.

Rule #2: You say, "I have no knowledge of this alleged debt."

Golden words

Those two words are golden and can save you from many a nightmare. ALLEGED DEBT.

You never, ever, ever claim the debt. Never acknowledge the debt. As I said earlier, chances are that it is not your debt.

When you say this, expect to get their ire. Their intimidation skills come out full force. More threats. More lies. More phony baloney stories of how he will come snatch your firstborn, and the litter of new puppies, and all the presents under your Christmas tree. (He's a mean one, Mr. Grinch.)

Again, your line is: "I have no knowledge of this alleged debt. Please send the account information in writing. I will look into my records."

Those are your lines. Practice them in the mirror. Memorize. Rehearse. You do not acknowledge the debt. Never admit to owing the debt. It may not be yours and even if it is, you may not owe it. We'll get to that in a minute.

When the thug calls, you say: "I have no knowledge of this alleged debt. Please send the account information in writing. I will look into my records."

Got it?

Then you hang up.

No chatty chatty

Don't stay on the line with the collection caller. Don't be chatty with them. You have three lines in this scene. "I have no knowledge of this alleged debt. Please send the account information in writing. I will look into my records."

If the collector is legit, they must contact you in writing when you request it. Sometimes—oftentimes—they will call repeatedly. Your script never changes: "I have no knowledge of this alleged debt."

Do not give them any ammunition to use against you. Wait it out. Silently. Time is on your side.

The debt may not be yours or it could have expired. Either way, stay mum, no matter how brutal it gets.

It happens all the time. The *Wall Street Journal* reported:

> *Caroline Black's hands were shaking when she hung up the phone last week after a man who said he was a debt collector screamed at her, called her a derogatory term and bullied*

her over a $625 debt that she said did not exist.

This came after a week of harassing and threatening phone calls he made to her cell phone, her mother's house and her workplace. Each day, he became more aggressive; one day he called 12 times.

These thugs are relentless in their pursuit for your money. They threaten to sue or they'll say they plan to send someone to your house to arrest you.

These thugs either call people with old debt hoping to trick them or people with bad credit hoping to trick them, too. They think fear will get you to cave and say, "Okay, shut up, I'll pay!"

Don't do it.

Scams

This kind of scam still goes on every day. Why? Because people freak out and think they have to pay. Now you know better.

> Tell them to stop calling and to put any requests in writing.

Even if you think it could be your debt, say nothing. Always say, "Alleged debt." Tell them to stop calling and to put any requests in writing.

Those are your rights. Use them.

You do not want to open up the payment ticking clock if the debt is indeed yours. Sometimes an old debt gets the attention of the collectors and they try to collect something before the statute of limitations runs out.

Statute of limitations

That's right. Statute of limitations. Those are two more magic words for your arsenal. If the collection thugs attack, you counterattack.

This little known secret tactic—and completely legal—to completely wipe out your debt does not need to be a secret! Every American should know how to protect themselves. So let's spread the word!

The banks and the creditors and the collection agencies, especially those vicious bulldog collection agencies, do not want you to know about this method. If ever there was a nugget that they "really don't want you to know about," this is one.

This secret is a gold mine. It does not matter how much your debt was—the dollar amount is not at issue. Maybe you had $2,000 or maybe you had $20,000. Maybe you had even more. The beautiful thing is that method allows you to be rid of that debt! Totally, 100% debt free, forever and ever, amen.

This cure alone has helped thousands of people save thousands of dollars.

Once you know it, you will never forget it. You always refer to any debt as alleged debt and you know the statute of limitations. That means they cannot collect because you legally do not owe it.

Frank's story

One *Debt Cures* reader was glad that this method came to his rescue. Frank Cavestani was being hounded by bill collectors, too. He was able to eliminate $5,000 in debt.

He says: "My wife had an old debt of about $400 and so did I. It was forgotten, gone, written off. The company wrote it off because I wasn't working. When I did start working again, I got my credit report and worked with a financial advisor to pay off anything I still owed. This debt was not on there because it had been wiped off."

Then sometime after that, Frank began receiving bills on this debt. "I got this bill, one for $2,537, and another that amounted to over $5,000 for these past debts. I said, well how can they do that? They haven't sent me anything in all this time. I called them and they said, "We're allowed to do that. The new consumer protection law that came out in June of 2011 allows us to go back to people we wrote off and send you a bill and you owe us the money." I somehow didn't feel right about that. It felt like the mafia collecting some old debt."

Frank was right that something was indeed not right. He was smart. "I wrote people. I wrote my congressman. I finally wrote the *New York Times* business office. They said it was interesting and would investigate the story. I gave them all the information I had written to Capital One. I wrote them, too, and their president, and didn't hear back from them. But the paper called me back and said, "They can't do this. Statute of limitations. If they haven't sent you a bill in over four years." And, it had been years, close to ten in fact. So they can't do it. When I got back to the company and told them this, they basically said, "Well, okay, then don't pay it.""

Nice scam if you can get away with it. Don't let them get away with it.

Frank said: "The statute of limitations in both their state and my state allows me to ignore this. I ignored it. I never heard from them again."

It was a huge relief. Frank continues: "I was able to eliminate over $5,000 in debt with a simple technique. I was very pleased because I had just cleared all my debts up and then, suddenly, I got this debt of $5,000. It was like the financial world was against me."

The financial world certainly isn't for us.

Frank was shocked to hear about a long ago debt. "I didn't even remember having a Capital One card. At first I thought it was some kind of fraud. But then they sent me copies of some of the past bills. And so, it was there. I remembered it. Then my wife remembered it was written off by them. I'm still not sure if there is any law on the books that says they can send notices now on these old accounts, but I am sure of the law that means I didn't have to pay it now."

Spread the word

Many folks are thankful for statute of limitations. Let everyone know. Frank tried to share his story with the country, so that other folks would not be duped into paying old debts. "If a law allows them to dredge up their old bills and send them to you, so be it. But if you pay even a dollar of that, you're into it. You owe them all of it. Our original debt was only about $800 and then after all those years, they now said it was $5,000."

Crazy.

Be smart. Be like Frank. Don't take it. Fight back. Call people, write people. Don't accept the debt and don't pay it. Frank's story "was featured in the *LA Times* and then put in other newspapers. If you go online it's all over the place. Another magazine called *Celebrity Magazine* from Beverly Hills interviewed me, too."

Thanks, Frank, for sharing your story to help others.

Debt does not hang over your head forever. It has an expiration date, called a statute of limitations. Most people have heard of a statute of limitations in other areas. If you get in a car accident, you have, for example, a three-year statute of limitations to sue the person that hit you. If you do not file a lawsuit within that window of opportunity, you are out of luck. You cannot decide ten years later to make an issue of it. Life goes on and people need to be able to carry on with their lives without a burden of possible court action always hanging over them.

The same principle applies to people who have debt in their pasts. They, and you, need to be able to carry on with their lives as well, without a burden of possible collection action always hanging over them. A statute of limitations on debt, therefore, exists for that very reason.

Out of luck

The creditors have a window of opportunity to pursue collection and when that window is up, they are out of luck. If a creditor has not collected his money from you in this amount of time, he is out of luck.

There is a statute of limitations on debt. That is why they try so hard when the time is about to expire. They know it, but they do not want you to know it.

It's a common scenario.

Say you racked up some debt in your life. We all do. You had the usual bills and were living paycheck to paycheck. Sound familiar? Then say you were hit with that all-American blow, "downsized" from your job.

Happened to a lot of people. In the months between finding a new job, you had to use you credit cards to buy some of the basics. Food, gas, whatever. You had to live.

Then you got another job. Relief! You started paying down the balance on the credit cards. It was daunting. The balance never seemed to change. You paid for months, but felt like you were getting nowhere.

Then say your kid got sick and you missed some work. The doctor bills started to pile up now, too. It was one of those merry-go-round rides that no one wants to be on, but we all find ourselves on at one time or another.

> **The thug is banking on the hope that you are not aware of this law…**

Time passed and you changed jobs and moved several times and life got busy. Those credit card bills became a part of your past. It happens. Not all paid off, but you did the best you could and things slipped through the cracks.

You have settled in and things are going well, when out of the blue, years later, you get a call from a collection agency.

The account is ancient history, long written off as uncollectible by the credit card company. Forgotten. The creditor had gotten its tax benefit by writing it off and you are now shocked to be contacted by a credit hound.

The thug is banking (literally banking) on the hope that you are not aware of this law about statute of limitations. I am amazed at how successful they are at keeping this knowledge secret. Maybe it is because there is not a federal law declaring a three-year statute like we have for most other things.

Know the rules

The IRS is held to a federal statute of limitations, too. For example, you filed your 2009 tax return by April 15, 2010. They have three years, until April 15, 2013, to question you or audit you on that return. If something is amiss on that return, after April 16, 2013, they are barred by the statute of limitations from adjusting your taxes.

For the statute of limitations on debt, each state sets the amount of years. In many states, it is just three years. What does this mean for you?

Say your last activity on the credit card account was in December 2010. If you live in a state with a three-year statute, by December 2013, that debt, that entire balance, is off limits to the credit card company and the collection agencies.

That debt, in full, is gone. Untouchable. You can be debt free, baby!

Of course, the players in this power game do not want anyone to know. They want to shake you down and make you pay. They are good at scaring you, but don't let them. You know the real deal, so don't give them the time of day.

Many times the creditor or the collection agency will contact you right before the statute period is about to blow. They want to cash in. Don't ever let them intimidate you.

Do you know what to do?

DO NOTHING.

Do not be swayed. They will try a variety of tactics to get to you. You don't take threats and you do not succumb to sweet talk (the collection agents try all kinds of ways to get to you). You don't take their bull. No matter how they spread it, it's all bull.

Whenever you get a call from a collection person, do not ever admit to the debt. The possibilities for error on their part are endless and they really don't give a hoot. They could have you mixed up with someone else. They could have the wrong account. Or in many cases, they could be trying to collect on old debt. No matter what, you stay mum. You cannot trust them so absolutely, positively, do not take whatever they tell you as the gospel truth.

There are countless cases of bogus calls and the debt is completely made up. They will sound bossy and smart and have some of your personal information to make them sound official. Stand firm.

Your tactic is to remain calm. That always throws collection scum for a loop. They are used to playing hard ball and don't know what to do when someone does not get flustered. You be brief, and be firm.

Firm and calm

Remember the magic words that you need to use first: Alleged debt.

Okay, so you have that line down. Now the twist is timing.

As the saying goes, timing in life is everything. You are aware that in your state, the statute of limitations on debt is three years. You know the deadline on this debt has passed (or is just about to pass) and there is nothing legally that the collector can do. It does not mean that they will stop calling.

They may be very aggressive.

Collection Creep: "Joe America, I have record of your debt to Bad Bozo Company in the amount of $10,000 and I demand payment of $1,000 immediately."

He may bark and whine and tap dance for all you care. You say your line about alleged debt and say goodbye.

If you know indeed that the statue is gone, you simply say, "The statute of limitations has expired. Goodbye."

You do not need to say anything more. If the debt is old, collection activity is barred.

Read me: DEBT IS ELIMINATED. Gone. Forever.

That ten grand is wiped away. That's a glorious feeling. The amount does not matter; if the time is up, that's that.

Do you see what a revelation this is?!

Eliminated!

This secret needs to be revealed to all of America. Countless people have paid on debts that legally they did not owe. Do not be one of them!

If you do not know the statute of limitations for your state, you can check online. We also included that information here in this book for you. The current statute of limitations for each state is included here for you at the end of the chapter. Know what the statute is for your state so you are armed and ready to take on the collection creeps if they should set their sights on you.

Many states have a three-year statute. Imagine, when the statute of limitations applies, your credit card debt is untouchable after just three short years! 100% of your debt totally eliminated.

Debt free! Just by knowing the magic words. Many a life has been changed by this one method alone. Sweet.

Now let's back up a step and not even have a collection agency creep in the picture. Let's make the story be that CurlyQ got sued for collection by the credit card company. Some creditors will do this even though the debt is expired. They think you will cave in and pay. They don't expect you to know about timing of statutes.

CurlyQ knew and she didn't cave. She went to the judge and sweetly stated, "Your honor, the statute of limitations has expired for this debt."

The judge replied, "Case dismissed."

Ah, two more magic words.

These strategies work. Do not pay on something that is not yours and do not pay on a debt that is no longer yours. Do not claim the debt to be yours—that can start the statute clock ticking again. That is why the words "alleged debt" are so powerful.

A creditor may call on debt that is old because they do not think you know anything about these rules. Now you do. See? Knowledge is power.

Knowledge is money.

Folks have released debt and felt the freedom.

We at Debt Cures get letters of wonderful success stories of having vanquished the credit collection creeps. Using these simple words can be life changing. People have eliminated thousands upon thousands of dollars of debt with this method alone.

It is really exciting.

A sample of what some people have said:

- ✔ This stuff works! I can't believe it! I got rid of ALL my debt!

- ✔ I no longer have credit card debt! Hooray!

- ✔ *Debt Cures* was the magic cure for me! Magic words! Love them! Thank you!

These methods work. Ask debt collectors like Marissa, she'll tell you. Ask people who have used these methods and had thousands of dollars wiped away. They'll tell you. Statute of limitations eliminates debt.

It's time to know all the stuff they—the government and the credit and bank creeps—don't want you to know.

We've included this table for you so you can see how quickly debt can disappear. This information is correct to the best of our knowledge as we go to print.

Be sure to check with an attorney or someone in your state that is knowledgeable in these areas, in case the number of years for expiry of your debt has changed, and for any other relevant information.

For more info or to see this chart online, go to

http://www.creditinfocenter.com/rebuild/statuteLimitations.shtml.

(Their fine print: The material provided in this table is for informational purposes only and should not be construed as legal advice. Although the material is deemed to be accurate and reliable, we do not make any representations as to its accuracy or completeness and as a result, there is no guarantee it is not without errors.)

State	Oral	Written	Promissory	Open-ended Accounts	State Statute: Open Accounts
AL	6	3	6	3	§6.2.37
AR	3	5	3	5	§4-3-118
AK	6	3	3	3	§09.10.053
AZ	3	6	6	6	HB 2412
CA	2	4	4	4	§337
CO	6	6	6	6	§13-80-103.5
CT	3	6	6	6	Chapter 926 Sec. 52-576
DE	3	3	3	3	Title 10 Sec.8106
DC	3	3	3	3	§12-301
FL	4	5	5	4	§95.11
GA	4	6	6	4**	§9-3-25
HI	6	6	6	6	HRS 657-1(4)
IA	5	10	5	10	§614.1.5
ID	4	5	5	5	§5-216
IL	5	10	10	5 or 10***	735 ILCS 5/13-206
IN	6	10	10	6	§34-11-2-9
KS	3	3	3	3	§60-512
KY	5	15	15	5 or 15	§413.120 & 413.090
LA	10	3	10	3	§2-3494-4
ME	6	6	6	6	§14-205-752
MD	3	3	6	3	§5-101
MA	6	6	6	6	§260-2
MI	6	6	6	6	§600.5807.8
MN	6	6	6	6	§541.05
MO	5	5	5	5	§516.120
MS	3	3	3	3	§15-1-29
MT	5	8	8	8	27-2-202
NC	3	3	5	3	§1-52.1
ND	6	6	6	6	28-01-16

State	Oral	Written	Promissory	Open-ended Accounts	State Statute: Open Accounts
NE	4	4	4	4	§25-206
NH	3	3	3	3	382-A:3-118
NJ	6	6	6	6	2A:14-1
NM	4	4	4	4	§37-1-4
NV	4	4	4	4	NRS 11.190
NY	6	6	6	6	§2-213
OH	6	6	6	6	§2305.07
OK	3	3 or 5	5	3 or 5	§12-95A(1), (2)
OR	6	6	6	6	§12.08
PA	4	4	4	4	42 Pa. C.S.5525(a)
RI	10	10	10	10	§6A-2-725
SC	10	10	3	3	SEC 15-3-530
SD	3	6	6	6	§15-2-13
TN	6	6	6	6	28-3-109
TX	4	4	4	4	§16.004
UT	4	6	6	4	78-12-25
VA	3	5	6	3	8.01-246
VT	6	6	5	6	§9A-3-118
WA	3	6	6	6	4.16.040
WI	6	6	10	6	893.43
WV	10	10	10	10	§55-2-6
WY	8	10	10	8	§1-3-105

** Georgia Court of Appeals came out with a decision on January 24, 2008 in Hill v. American Express that in Georgia the statute of limitations on a credit card is six years after the amount becomes due and payable.

*** An Illinois appeals court ruled on May 20, 2009, that the statute of limitations on a credit card debt without a written contract was 5 years.

Do NOT pay an account that is expired. For more information on time barred debts—debt you no longer have to pay—see http://www.creditinfocenter.com/rebuild/statuteLimitations.shtml.

CHAPTER 10

Attack Identity Theft

"Identity theft continues to be one of the fastest growing crimes in the United States."
—Identity Theft Resource Center

Do you need a quick reminder of just a few of the magic words that you have learned already?

You probably recall from the last chapter the biggies of alleged debt and statute of limitations.

Don't forget the magic words of credit reports—file disputes.

See what you forgot already?

As you know, credit reports are the make-or-break paper of the financial world. There is another dose of magic words that assists in that arena, too. These words are all too common these days.

Another telling tale

I often tell the old story of my friend, Kurt. He applied for a credit card and was rejected. He was shocked to be rejected because he had an excellent credit history. Kurt went round and round with the credit card company trying to explain his good credit.

They finally told him why he was rejected. Kurt was informed that his application was declined because the credit report showed a $15,000 balance on an American Express account that had never been paid.

Kurt knew there had to be some kind of mistake. He had never, ever, had an American Express account.

Kurt made repeated phone calls to tell the credit card company that the debt was not his and never was. He told them that he had never had an American Express card so he could not possibly owe a dime, let alone $15,000.

They told him: "I'm sorry, sir, but your credit report shows you have an outstanding unpaid balance of $15,000 and we cannot issue you an account with our company."

Now do you see why you need to get your credit report and review it frequently? Mystery items can happen to anyone at any time. If Kurt would have requested his annual free reports, he would have seen this item.

Kurt sent letters explaining that he did not owe the $15,000 to American Express or any other creditor. He kept saying, "It's not mine."

What he needed to say to get their attention, what they finally responded to, were the two words: Identity Theft.

Identity theft affects MILLIONS of Americans. Just about everyone is touched in some way, at some time. The Federal Trade Commission states that over a million people are affected each and every year.

Identity theft does not appear to be waning. You need to learn to be safe and smart with your information.

Don't fall for the old tricks. Take a few precautions:

- ✔ Don't give out your private information over the phone unless you have called them yourself and are sure of whom you are speaking to.

- ✔ Never give sensitive info over a cell phone.

- ✔ Be cautious about using your credit card online. Know the site and know that it is secure.

- ✔ When doing financial transactions on your computer, do it from your home computer only. Do not do anything on a work computer or a laptop in a public place.

- ✔ Always shut down the computer when you are done.

- ✔ Only use your ATM card at your bank or trusted locations.

- ✔ Use a shredder at home to destroy your sensitive papers.

- ✔ Use the security software on your computer.

Identity thieves are alive and well, and up to new tricks all the time. They don't have to steal your purse to steal your information.

You may not know something is fishy until you check your credit report and see something that is not yours or you may get a call from the Fraud Department of your bank or credit company who found something suspicious.

No one knows exactly when or how the thief gets the information. These bad guys are genius. Too bad they don't use their cleverness for better endeavors. They could put people on Mars and cure cancer.

Protect your information

Protect your Social Security Number and your credit card and bank account information. A little bit of precaution goes a long way. According to the Huffington Post, you are even more likely to be taken advantage of during the holiday season.

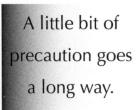
A little bit of precaution goes a long way.

You are using your cards more often and there are many seasonal workers who are not screened and vetted as well as some employers normally do. You are also using your card more often during the holidays, so it goes into more hands, increasing the odds of a security breach somewhere along the way. Your credit card may be getting copied via a handheld skimmer or a cell phone picture.

Pay attention when you hand over your card. Watch the clerk and do not be distracted by idle chit chat. During the holidays, more people open store charge cards to get that extra discount. That means you are giving out your personal information. That sensitive information, if not fully protected or destroyed, can be copied, leaving you open to identity theft.

People shop online more during the holidays, again opening themselves up to more opportunities for creeps to find their private information. Some sites may not be safe, but in the rush of the holidays, you go ahead and make a purchase anyway.

Also, many people are making online purchases when they are out and about. According to Huffington Post: "Surfing on an unsecured network can put you at risk for identity theft via "sidejacking." Programs like Firesheep allow someone to capture cookies transmitted over a public Wi-Fi connection and use those cookies to gain access to the unsecured e-mail and social networking accounts of anyone using the network. Once they have access to this information they can obtain the financial information you've provided those sites. Make sure you are using encrypted sites like Gmail to prevent this and know that this can also happen to your smartphone when switching from 3G to a wireless hotspot. To help protect your phone, turn on its encryption settings."

They go on to say: "Smartphone owners are a third more likely to become identity theft victims than the general public due to "careless consumer usage." During the holidays, consumers can become more inclined to multi-task and take care of personal information (paying bills, etc.) on their phone as they wait in long checkout lines. Others may forget their phone at a bar or party, or set it down on a store shelf while grabbing an item they want to purchase. The amount of personal data and the ability to access financial information through apps on your phone can mean your identity is more likely to get stolen if you lose your phone."

Be vigilant

Besides all the new high-tech ways to get your information, when you are out in the holiday rush, there are more crowds and more opportunity for a good old-fashioned purse stealer or pickpocket. The bad guys still operate low tech, too.

No matter, all throughout the year, review your credit report so you are not caught off guard like my friend all those years ago, when identity theft was still a new thing. If something is fishy, report it right away.

Identity theft is not a new thing. It grows every year. Reports of filings go up every year. The latest reports are that identity theft costs Americans over $1.5 billion a year.

The FTC provides helpful information. Their web site states ways you may notice that your information has been stolen:

- ✔ You see withdrawals from your bank account that you can't explain.

- ✔ You don't get your bills or other mail.

- ✔ Merchants refuse your checks.

- ✔ Debt collectors call you about debts that aren't yours.

- ✔ You find unfamiliar accounts or charges on your credit report.

- ✔ Medical providers bill you for services you didn't use.

- ✔ Your health plan rejects your legitimate medical claim because the records show you've reached your benefits limit.

- ✔ A health plan won't cover you because your medical records show a condition you don't have.

- ✔ The IRS notifies you that more than one tax return was filed in your name, or that you have income from an employer you don't work for.

- ✔ You get notice that your information was compromised by a data breach at a company where you do business or have an account.

If you are a victim, get busy repairing your credit right away. The government provides sample letters and forms that can help you exercise your rights as an identity theft victim, like requesting action from the credit reporting companies and businesses where the thief opened new accounts or tampered with your existing ones.

You can download these at http://www.consumer.ftc.gov/articles/0281-sample-letters-and-forms-victims-identity-theft.

You can get FTC Identity Theft Victim's Complaint and Affidavit at http://www.consumer.ftc.gov/articles/pdf-0094-identity-theft-affidavit.pdf.

To take action right away to protect your credit, you can stop an identity thief from doing more damage. Follow these three steps as soon as possible:

✔ Place an Initial Fraud Alert

✔ Order Your Credit Reports

✔ Create an Identity Theft Report

Calls and letters

It is a pain in the arse if you are a victim of identity theft. Resolving identity theft takes phone calls and letters. Create a system to organize your papers and calls, and to track deadlines.

> Create a system to organize your papers and calls...

Create a log of all telephone calls. Record the date of each call and the names and telephone numbers of everyone you contact. Prepare your questions before you call. Write down the answers.

Send letters by certified mail. Ask for a return receipt. Use the sample letters and forms. Create a filing system. Keep all originals.

Send copies of your documents and reports, not originals. Make copies of your identification to include in letters.

Placing both extended fraud alerts and credit freezes on your credit reports can make it more difficult for an identity thief to open new accounts in your name.

You can get step-by-step instructions for disputing fraudulent charges and accounts related to identity theft. Go to http://www. consumer.ftc.gov/articles/0290-repairing-your-credit-after-iden-tity-theft.

Federal law limits your liability if your credit, ATM, or debit card is lost or stolen, but your liability may depend on how quickly you report the loss or theft. Report it right away, the sooner, the better for you.

Keep your children's information safe, too. A child's Social Security number can be used by identity thieves to apply for government benefits, open bank and credit card accounts, apply for a loan or utility service, or rent a place to live.

Check for a credit report to see if your child's information is being misused. Take immediate action if it is.

Besides the FTC, you can go to the Identity Theft Resource Center for assistance. Visit http://www.idtheftcenter.org/. You can also use the United States' Department of Justice at http://www. justice.gov/criminal/fraud/websites/idtheft.html.

CHAPTER 11

Medical Mysteries Solved

*"Medical bills are one of the top three reasons that
people file for bankruptcy."*
—Bankruptcy attorney

The number one cause of bankruptcy in this country continues to be medical bills. Over 60% of people who file bankruptcy do so because their health created such debt and they could not pay it.

This is not the place for a debate on Obama care. This is the place to find relief from what ails you, and for many people, it is those gosh darn medical bills that keep piling up.

A hospital stay can be a life saver, and a real killer, if you get my drift. Once a person gets out of the hospital, sometimes the real nightmare begins—the nightmare of dealing with the bills. Over 44 million people are paying on medical bills. One in five American families was having trouble paying off their medical debt.

Medical bill collectors are the king of the thugs. They are notorious for going for the kill. They show no mercy. You don't want to be turned over to medical collections.

Consider your medical bills a priority because the medical industry certainly does. Do not ignore them. The first thing to do is to review every line item. Go over the bills with a fine-tooth comb.

The hospitals and insurance companies quite often make errors on the statements and it is up to you to find them.

Review everything

Question anything and everything that does not make sense to you. When you do reach an agreement, keep records of all phone calls and maintain notes with dates and names of who you talked to. Keep a log book of every call, every letter, every word.

If you are having trouble making the payments, give them a call right away. As with all debt, you can negotiate medical bills, too. Right now, especially medical bills.

Point blank: Ask for a better payment arrangement.

> As with all debt, you can negotiate medical bills, too.

Maybe you need to make a lesser payment this month, but can pay more next month. Maybe you simply need to lower the amount of the monthly payments. Whatever your situation, ask and you usually will receive.

Talk to them. Never let it go. If you are already to the point of collection, negotiate. Do not back down. If you can pay a certain amount, they may consider the entire outstanding balance paid in full.

Pick up the phone and ask. You may be surprised at how willing the other side is to work with you.

CNN reported on a doctor who negotiated his own medical bills down, too! Talk to your doctor. Deal with the doctor directly. He or she may be more likely to take a payment arrangement or a partial payment. Getting something is better than nothing. Not having to hassle with insurance and collectors is nice for both sides.

Talk to the doctor upfront, before any surgery or treatment happens. You can arrive at a deal and avoid the sticker shock of the bills. If you do not have health insurance, talk to the doctor! The docs want to get paid and if there is no insurance company involved, they can talk directly with you. You are the one to pay so you are the one they want to work with. Make them work for you. You can work out a payment arrangement even before you have any services rendered.

Negotiate

Times are tough and the doctors, like everyone else, just want to get paid. Now more than ever, the other party is willing to work with you. If there is no way you can pay the full fee, tell them up front. Negotiate. That is a word you better learn from *Debt Cures*.

Always, negotiate. The one perfect magic word that you must always keep in your mind: ASK!

Insurance companies sometimes act like they rule the world. They can take up a lot of your time and energy when you are trying to figure out your medical bills.

I know a guy who had a situation with his medical bills that drove him nuts, until he fired off these new magic words. Yep, more magic words.

Bill had cancer, and now had to fight the insurance folks. The billing wars began. He went round and round with them, and wound up all wound up, completely frustrated. Over the course of his hospital stays, his bills mounted up to nearly a million dollars.

Ch-ching. That is enough to give a guy a heart attack, and yet not unusual for a hospital stay these days. That's another thing that is completely out of whack in this country, the cost of every little thing they charge you for at the hospital.

Bill was talking to the insurance company about some items the insurance company was not paying. The hospital was hounding Bill for the money, about fifty grand. Bill was hounding the insurance company, to no avail.

This scenario involved some medication and a hospital stay that the insurance company claimed was not covered. Bill spent hours on the phone with the insurance representative.

More magic words

Then he used the new magic words: "I am recording this call."

Instantly, the insurance rep changed her tone.

Bill said it was like a miracle.

Suddenly, the paperwork was found. After all the game playing, the insurance representative had the needed paperwork that showed the medication and the hospital stay were approved and proper.

Holy cow.

Bill had spent hours trying to straighten out the mess, and suddenly with one magic phrase, all it took was five minutes, the paperwork appeared and the proper address to mail the checks was found.

He did not have to pay those bills. Thousands upon thousands of dollars off his back. Try it. It's an easy one. "I am recording this call."

Right now, unemployment is still at an all-time high so there are many people who are without health benefits.

Don't despair if you are one of them. You can still have safe medical care and not go broke in the process.

> You never know what you can get until you ask.

There are places that help you find insurance that is affordable or maybe even free. Go online and look up various resources that help people find healthcare such as Healthcare Advocacy, Patient Advocate Foundation, and Patient Services Incorporated.

If you had medical benefits at your old job, you can continue on with that policy under COBRA. You have the same coverage, but you have to pay the premiums now instead of your employer. All employers have to offer COBRA, but maybe the price of the premiums is too steep, especially since you just lost your job.

Statistics show that only about 10% of laid off employees pay the COBRA premiums. Many times it is cheaper to go get your own insurance policy than to pay the COBRA cost.

If you are looking for health insurance, compare policies and prices online at ehealthinsurance.com. If you are self-employed, you know how expensive health coverage can be. Never forget to negotiate. You never know what you can get until you ask. Right? What is the one easy magic word? ASK!

Health Magazine reports that some agencies provide help for medical care. Talk to the social worker at the hospital and check online for United Way's referral guide. You can also check out:

HealthWell Foundation

This nonprofit organization helps needy patients pay their insurance premiums, as well as prescription drug and other out-of-pocket costs. You can apply online (your doctor needs to fill out a form, too) for up to a year's assistance. After that, you'll need to reapply.

Patient Access Network Foundation

For U.S. residents who are being treated for one of 21 diseases on this organization's list—which includes breast cancer, cystic fibrosis, and multiple sclerosis—Patient Access offers $1,500 to $8,500 of assistance toward medication costs for one year. You'll hear back on your online application within 48 business hours.

Chronic Disease Fund

This fund provides help for prescription drug co-payments for chronic disease or cancer patients. Typically, patients receive $2,500 to $8,000 of aid per calendar year. If you choose to use a pharmacy associated with the fund, you can avoid having to submit claims for reimbursement.

Patient Advocate Foundation

If you're insured, Patient Advocate can help with your pharmaceutical co-payments. The foundation offers assistance to those with diseases such as diabetes, osteoporosis, rheumatoid arthritis, and various cancers.

UnitedHealthcare Children's Foundation

This organization helps families with insurance plans that don't fully cover their children's needs. For instance, it pays for speech therapy and hearing aids that families typically have to pay for out-of-pocket. Only those with a commercial health benefit plan—and not a federally funded plan like Medicaid—can qualify.

Drugs

One of the biggest expenses of health care is prescription drugs. Drug costs can be outrageous. Many people need insurance coverage just for the drug benefits.

Now many drug stores and supermarkets have pharmacies that offer programs for $4 generic drugs. Make sure that your doctor gives the prescription and checks that generics are approved, too.

Many states also offer discount drug programs. See what your state has to offer. Most take applications for relief programs at the same time as filing your state tax return. Senior citizens and low income folks most certainly need to look into these programs.

Look into these assistance and advocate programs as well:

- ✔ HealthWell Foundation
- ✔ FamilyWize discount drug card
- ✔ Needy Meds
- ✔ Rx Assist
- ✔ Rx Hope
- ✔ Chronic Disease Fund
- ✔ Partnership for Prescription Assistance
- ✔ The Access Project

Organizations and Foundations

There is also financial assistance available from the foundations of various diseases. If you have a certain type of ailment, research to see if there are funds available to offset your medical expenses.

These places offer several programs that help qualifying patients pay for health insurance premiums, prescription medicines and other treatment-related expenses.

Many organizations do have financial aid:

- ✔ Heart Disease: Heart Support of America
- ✔ Kidney Disease: American Kidney Fund
- ✔ HIV/AIDS: The Access Project
- ✔ Hepatitis: The Access Project
- ✔ Vision Care: EyeCare America and Vision USA
- ✔ Caring Voice Coalition
- ✔ National Organization for Rare Diseases

Besides patient assistance programs, take advantage of going to a free clinic when you need health care. There are federally funded health care centers in rural areas and urban communities. Your tax dollars fund these clinics, so you need to be aware that they exist. If you are in between jobs and do not have health insurance, you simply pay what you are able to afford. The clinic has a sliding scale and you are charged based upon your income.

These health centers provide:

- ✔ checkups when you're well
- ✔ treatment when you're sick
- ✔ complete care when you're pregnant
- ✔ immunizations and checkups for your children
- ✔ dental care and prescription drugs for your family
- ✔ mental health and substance abuse care if you need it

For more information and how to find a health care clinic, visit findahealthcenter.hrsa.gov. Type in your address and click the "Find Health Centers" button to find health centers near you.

If you are looking for work, don't forget about part-time jobs. These jobs may not be what you are looking for long-term, but in the short-term, many employers provide benefits to part-time employees, including health care. If you need a job to get by, try to find a job with benefits as opposed to no benefits. It only makes sense.

Some of the companies that offer benefits to part-timers include: Aerotek, JCPenney, JP Morgan Chase, Kaplan, Lowe's, Land's End, REI, Starbucks, Nordstrom's, Target, Trader Joe's, U-Haul, UPS, Whole Foods.

Many hospitals and universities also employ people on a part-time basis and provide benefits like medical insurance.

> ... take advantage of going to a free clinic when you need health care.

We always get a second opinion on medical advice, and since you know it is good to comparison shop for items you buy, put two and two together. Compare doctors and their prices just like any other service you use.

If you have a health savings account through your employer, use it. If your employer provides some kind of health club deal, do it. If your company offers a quit-smoking program, take it. Smokers can be charged higher insurance premiums, so if you want to kick the habit, you'll save money from not buying a pack a day and you'll save in health costs.

Don't let medical bills pile up and don't let medical bills get you down.

Use these tactics and your medical bills will become part of your medical history, and your financial history.

CHAPTER 12

Credit Card Update

*"Credit card debt stands at a distressing
and startling number."*
—nerdwallet.com

How bad is it?

Pretty bad.

The latest stats as we go to print (and it seems the ticker tape keeps ticking higher every second) tally up as follows:

- ✔ Average credit card debt: $15,112
- ✔ Average mortgage debt: $146,215
- ✔ Average student loan debt: $31,240

Average credit card debt is over $15,000. How do you rank? Are you among the "average"?

In total, American consumers owe:

- ✔ $11.08 trillion in debt
- ✔ $846.9 billion in credit card debt

- ✔ $7.75 trillion in mortgages
- ✔ $1,002 billion in student loans

An increase of 10.9% from last year.

And the government tries to tell us that we are on the rebound and the economy is recovering? Do you see it? Do you feel it? Do the numbers reflect a better position? It does not appear that way.

Credit card debt is out of control and has been. It is really crazy that student loan debt has taken over the #2 spot. Of course, mortgage debt is higher. That makes sense, a house, a large asset, carries a large price tag. College does, too, and folks cannot afford it. So student loan debt sky rockets.

How do people pay for stuff when things get tight? With credit cards.

Look at these numbers from the Federal Reserve:

	Total Credit Card Debt	Average Household Credit Card Debt	Average Indebted Household Debt	
October 2012	$857.6 billion	$7,193	$15,418	
Change from September 2012	+0.66%	+0.59%	+0.59%	
Change from October 2011	+1.05%	+0.23%	+0.23%	
Change from September 2012 (annualized)	+7.90%	+7.07%	+7.07%	

Household debt keeps going up, and yet the talking heads tell us things are improving. I'll believe it when the numbers show it. People are using credit cards to make ends meet, not to boost the economy with "increased consumer confidence."

Consumer confidence has long left the station.

MORE households now have credit card debt than even two short years ago. Where is the confidence, Mr. President? Not here.

What is also interesting to note: Any decrease in indebtedness is NOT due to repayment. It is due to default. Ain't that a grand state of affairs?

Credit card companies gave up and wrote off a large number of defaulted accounts. These charge-offs account for the reduction in overall debt. It was not that the money fell from the sky and people were able to repay their credit cards.

The money tree has dropped its leaves.

Improvement?

At year-end 2012, average credit card debt was increasing and so was the number of late payments. Things did not get much better in the following years. The numbers are looking pretty much the same. Probably the same for this year.

Also of note, *USA Today* reported that at year-end 2012, credit card companies are needing business so they are issuing cards now a lot more loosely that in recent years when everything tightened up.

They are now giving credit cards to nonprime borrowers. Does anyone feel a deja vu coming on? About one-third of new cards issued were to borrowers with scores considered nonprime.

USA Today states, "Banks have become more open to issuing credit cards to higher-risk borrowers due to tight competition for top-rated consumers, many of whom are not signing up for additional credit."

They will get business any way they can, be it to folks who cannot pay or who will struggle to repay. What does that mean for the banks? The ability to charge fees and penalties. That's how they make their money.

> ...credit card debt delinquency carries more weight on your credit score...

We Americans have over six million credit cards in our pockets and purses. That is six million credit card statements that need to get paid.

Pay 'em.

Those credit creeps want your money, in every back alley way they can get it. Not only do you avoid fees and penalties when you pay on time, you are also protecting your credit score. The Consumer Financial Protection Bureau's (CFPB) report states that credit card debt delinquency carries more weight on your credit score than other kinds of debt, like student loans and the mortgage.

Breakdown shakedown

The CFPB report shows the breakdown: Credit card companies supply most of the information that goes into your credit report. Fifty-eight percent of the pieces of information contained in the average credit report are furnished by credit card issuers.

The rest: Thirteen percent are supplied by debt-collection agencies. Seven percent come from education lenders, another seven from mortgage lenders, and the remaining are provided by creditors that make auto loans.

In the CFPB report, using Vantage Score calculations, if you have a credit score of 760, being 60 days late on a credit card payment will cause you to lose 70-90 points, the same amount as being behind on a mortgage or car payment.

But since each late card payment counts against you separately, and people tend to have multiple cards, the cards often carry more weight. In other words, being behind on your credit card payments matters more to your credit score than your consistency in repaying bigger debts, such as home and student loans.

You have more credit cards, thus more opportunities to get dinged.

One news report stated: "The CFPB report, the first the agency has issued about credit scorers, didn't say companies had broken the law in their evaluations of creditworthiness. But it did raise red flags about the accuracy of credit scores."

Tell us something we don't already know.

Same old song and dance. Are you sick of it yet?

We already talked about credit scores so we know what to do. It may not seem like you have any power when you read reports and statistics, but let me remind you that you do.

It sure as heck seems like the banks and the credit card companies want to lord their power over us. They will try. They want us to think that we are powerless in their shadow.

But they're wrong.

YOU have the power.

Confidence

You have to believe it and you have to flaunt your power. Strap on that confidence and pick up the phone. They want consumer confidence? We got it!

Always, always, always, the more you know, the more power you have. Take for example, ATM fees. You can choose to pay the fee, sometimes three bucks or more, or you can go find a machine in your bank system, or go to the grocery store or gas station and use your debit card.

Don't give the banks these fees!

Can you imagine if you did that all the time? What could you do with an extra thirty bucks a week? That's $120 a month. That's a payment on a credit card. It could be groceries or dinner out. It could be a lot of things.

So pay attention and do not just give your money away to the banks for the "convenience" of using their ATM machine.

Key words: Pay attention. Pay attention to your statements. Many people don't even look at them. Always review the charges to be sure that they are yours. Also, look at the fee section on the statement.

Were you hit with:

- ✔ Late payment fee?
- ✔ Over limit fee?
- ✔ Annual fee?
- ✔ Increase in interest rate?
- ✔ Any other kind of crazy fee?

Earlier we talked about negotiating everything, and you can. Absolutely. Negotiate everything. One of your magic words is ASK!

Another is: DEMAND.

This Debt Cure came from a reader, Tom. Tom was haggling with the customer service representative of his credit card company.

He had read the first *Debt Cures*, so he knew to pick up the phone and call and ask for removal of fees.

After several minutes of conversation, the Customer Service representative said, "Sir, are you simply asking for the removal of these fees or are you demanding?"

Being the smart man that he is, Tom picked up on the subtle nuance and replied that he was demanding.

That's all it took. A simple demand. His late fees and the accompanying interest fees were immediately wiped off his account balance.

Demand

Add that to your list of powerful magic words. Demand. When Tom said "demand," his late fees were waived. This technique is a little bit of a finesse item. Some credit card companies will respond to you asking for the removal of fees. Ask and you shall receive.

However, some may treat your polite, but firm, asking as something they are supposed to counter. You should be able to tell after conversing with the customer service representative for a few minutes which way you think you should proceed.

Credit card companies are always changing their policies, so feel out the person on the other end of the line. It may be obvious how they are treating your query or they may even give you the golden opportunity and ask you point blank if you are demanding.

That gives them an out. The phone center rep can then write in their comments or notes something to the effect that "the customer demanded the fees be waived or they would close their account. In order to keep the customer, I waived the late fees."

If you get no assistance from the customer service rep, ask to speak to the supervisor. Or should I say, demand to speak to the supervisor.

Another phrase to add to your tool box is another simple yet powerful technique. This works well in all kinds of situations, from your creditors to your kids. No matter what the circumstance, frame your query with these magic words: Would you be willing?

Would you be willing?

Any question, or demand, can be couched with those first four words. Would you be willing to discuss the late fee on my statement? Would you be willing to remove those fees? Would you be willing to lower my interest rate? Would you be willing to give me another month to pay? Would you be willing to delete that from my account? Would you be willing to consider taking a lower payment?

For those customer service reps who are not going to cater to your demands, you can work it with the "would you be willing" way instead.

The possibilities are endless. Countless negotiations can begin with these four words. Try it and see what results you get.

There is another magic sentence, as well, to add to your arsenal: Is that the best you can do?

If you are negotiating a better interest rate on your credit card, simply ask, "Is that the best you can do?"

Keep at them until they point blank say that it is the best they can do. You write it down for your records. Negotiate anything and everything in this way, not just your credit card payments and issues.

Is that the best you can do?

If you are buying a car or booking a hotel room, simply ask, "Is that the best you can do?" This one sentence cuts through the haggle and hassle and gets down to the bottom line. You want to get the best deal every time. So ask for it. And sometimes, demand it.

> ...lower your rate, you are saving yourself money.

I get tremendous feedback from folks who read my books. Probably the number one thing that garnered the largest response from the *Debt Cures* books was how easy these methods really are. And that they work.

People don't believe until they try it. And then they are amazed at the results and sometimes feel like kicking themselves for waiting so long to try these techniques. I'm not kidding—these methods work!

The favorite is the simple phone trick. Nothing up my sleeve. Nothing in my hat. Just a telephone is all I need to make debt disappear. The people who try it love it. I get comments all the time, everywhere I go.

"Kevin, it worked! I called my credit card company and they lowered my rate! Thank you!"

Shelly B. was hounded by debt collectors, was in debt about $30,000. Shelly was able to apply the methods in the book and negotiate her debt. She says, "I mean, it's step by step and it's easy as 123. Negotiating crazy interest rates and eliminating late fees, "I was able to save $800 a month using the methods in the *Debt Cures* book. And, over a year I was able to eliminate $7,000 worth of debt by using the book."

I love when folks apply these tactics and get to keep money in their pocket instead of the credit card industry coffers.

Every time you lower your rate, you are saving yourself money. Every percentage point you lower equates to less debt you pay back. You can save hundreds and thousands of dollars. That is worth a simple phone call to say, "Would you be willing…"

Hundreds and thousands of dollars. You can have it. Or they can. What are you waiting for?

Success

Paul writes: *"I was able to successfully negotiate with my credit card lenders. Bank of America brought my rate down from 28% to 4.25% and Chase Bank brought my interest rate down from 22% to 6.5%."*

Do you have any idea how much that saved Paul?

Paul also said: *"The book gave me the insight, knowledge, and confidence to call and the correct verbiage to use in my negotiations."*

Correct verbiage = magic words.

Amber writes: *"This is one of the most useful books I have ever read. I am now helping all my friends and family. I called my credit card companies and literally dropped my interest rate from 31% down to 10%. I have called for my friend and got 15% down to 1%. It is amazing."*

Amazing indeed. A phone call. Do it.

Sam wrote: *"I negotiated a credit card from 26.99% down to 0% for five months and then it will be 9.99%."*

0%. Nice.

I get letters all the time. 28% down to 4.5%. 30% down to 11%. 22% down to 6.5%. What is your letter going to say?

Banks and credit card companies don't advertise it but they are reducing principal balances, not just interest rates, in some cases. They know that something is better than nothing, so if you have been delinquent for a few months, call them up and ask for a principal reduction. Odds are that they will consider it. This economy is not letting up.

There are many ways to cut your credit card debt. You can start right now. Get out your iPad, your phone, your computer, your checkbook, whatever.

Something as simple as paying twice the minimum payment on your credit card statement can cut your debt instantly. And, it takes only an instant to do it. Don't wait. Don't dread paying the bills. Don't put it off.

Run the numbers

A little known web site can show you exactly how you can cut your credit card bills in an instant. People are astounded. Try it yourself.

Go to http://debtdestroyer.tv. Type in your credit card balance, interest rate, monthly payment. Hit submit. BAM!

You will see how much you save, simply by doubling that payment.

For example, say you have $10,000 with a rate of 11.99% and you make a monthly payment of $400 on that debt. Let this site compute for you to see what you save if all you do is make a higher monthly payment.

> ...making twice the minimum payment, you cut your bills dramatically.

Assume you have debt of $25,000 and you pay an interest rate of 14.99% with a monthly payment of $350. That is not enough to pay off that debt, even if you paid for 100 years. If you double that payment to $700, you can have it paid off in just shy of four years.

A hundred years or four years? Doubling your monthly payment makes a huge difference and saves you huge amounts of money.

You can also use the CNN Money debt reduction planner at http://cgi.money.cnn.com/tools/debtplanner/debtplanner.jsp. Find out how long it will take to become debt free and how much you'll pay in interest by making just the minimum monthly payments. We love to show people how by simply making twice the minimum payment, you cut your bills dramatically.

Simple to save

It is simple to use, too. You type in all your credit card balances and the interest rates and the minimum payments. You then can choose to see what happens if you pay a certain amount each month. It is amazing to see in dollars and cents how much you save.

You can also type in a timeframe that you want to be debt free. Say that you want your credit cards paid off in two years. This CNN Money planner calculates for you how much you need to pay each month.

They also provide a pie chart showing how much money goes to principal and how much goes to interest. A picture paints a thousand words.

Your plan summary also gives a strategy and what to do first.

Easy peasy.

What are you waiting for?

Use the technology at your fingertips and the quick, easy methods to get going. You can use your bank site to pay or you can go to the credit card site itself and make a payment. You can use your old fashioned checkbook and pay via snail mail.

You don't have to wait until the due date. Be inspired NOW to take action. Take control of your credit cards. Do something today.

CHAPTER 13

Fast Money

"Bank your sperm." One way to make fast money.
—The internet

Yep. That's one way to make fast money.

There are hundreds. People do not have to be slaves to the job or boss to make money. That place where you go to work is just one chunk of many chunks of cash available to you. Thinking differently can help you live differently.

Times are tough and the economy is not recovering like they say. You can sit around and wait for Mr. Obama and the feds to give you some kind of bailout, like that's gonna happen, or you can put on your thinking cap and make some fast money yourself.

That money is yours to spend, on bills, on debt, on credit cards, on whatever. Now more than ever, people need ways to come up with some cash and come up with it quickly. Are you in a jam? Need some immediate relief to a pressing problem or money issue? Just want some extra cash?

Whatever your situation, I don't know anybody who doesn't want to make some extra bucks and do it easily and get practically immediate results. Even if you are not in debt, extra money is always a worthwhile venture.

If you start to think on it, you can come up with ways to bring in a little dough. Ask your friends. I bet they can come up with ten ways to make money without really lifting a finger. Well, maybe a finger, but no heavy lifting involved. No time consuming start-ups and no inventory to stock and no monetary investments.

Fast money is not about going back to school or building a business, although those are absolutely great ideas.

Start quick and easy.

✔ **Recycle**. Yes, cash in those cans. Do a roundup of your neighborhood, scavenge, be a dumpster diver if you want. It doesn't take long to accumulate a bunch of cans. If you live near a park or beach or anywhere people gather, you can find tons (well, maybe not a ton) quickly. See how quickly you make a hundred bucks from this. It doesn't have to be just cans. Do a neighborhood drive-through on garbage night to collect any kind of scrap metal.

✔ **Resell**. Be the go-to guy for tickets. Scoop tickets to hot events in your area (or anywhere with the internet) and turn around and sell them for a slight profit. Maybe you even take a commission for buying the tickets for friends in the first place. You be the guy calling or onlining to get the concert or sporting event tickets and get paid for that time and effort. Any leftover tickets, post on Facebook or craigslist or StubHub.

✔ **Grown Up Lemonade Stand.** Go to where people are and sell them what they need. Sell water at a parade or sporting event parking lot (if legal). Stand on the street corner and at the traffic light offering a drink or a flower or some easy-to-sell items to motorists. A cold soda on a hot day with no waiting at a drive-through. Genius.

✔ **Plasma.** Most places do not pay for blood, although some do, but they do pay for plasma. What's the difference? Ask a scientist. Call your blood bank to see what donations they pay for.

✔ **Life Insurance.** Many life insurance policies have a cash value. If you need the cash now, call your agent and cash out. It usually does not affect your premium.

✔ **Rent a Room.** Or your couch. Take in a regular boarder or take in visitors. Internet places like coachsurfing have made it popular to let people crash on your couch. You can do your own version with people who know people you know and make a little side cash.

✔ **Sell Your Time Share.** Do you have a condo in Cabo? A villa at Disney World? A room at some golf resort? Sell it! You will get more bang for your buck by unloading the property. There is no sense paying the annual maintenance on something you are not living in. When you want to go to such places, rent a room or stay with a friend or find a deal using the creative thought processes you learn in this book.

✔ **Rent Your Time Share.** Not sure if you want to sell that time share condo or vacation home on the lake? Rent it out! You can still have use of it when you want it, and you can collect big bucks from others who will be able to enjoy it too.

✔ **Sell Your Body for Science.** Not really. The labs may or may not pay for your cadaver, but you want the money now. Some research places need people to test vaccines and other studies, and they will pay. Check out National Institute of Health.

- ✔ **Get a Temp Job.** Let the temp service do the legwork of finding a place for you to show up to show off your skills. You decide how many days you want to work. A great way to make good part-time money. Some places offer a real job, too, if you want it.

- ✔ **Good Old Fashioned Yard Sale.** If you have not used it, worn it, or even knew you had it, it's time to say goodbye and hello to cash. Rummage through the house and host a rummage sale.

- ✔ **Make Returns.** As you go through the closets looking for stuff to sell, you may find items you bought that still have the tags on them. Take them back to the store. If you do not have receipts, if you paid with your credit card, many store systems can trace the purchase and refund what you paid. Fast easy money.

- ✔ **Change jar.** Do you have one? Have you noticed how easy it is to simply use the dollar bills and let the change go into the change jar every night? Have you tallied up how fast that pile of coins adds up? Nice money, no hassle.

- ✔ **Find an online job.** The internet has created many opportunities. One legit one is Amazon Mechanical Turk. Companies post simple jobs and you choose what task you want to complete. When done, payment is put into your Amazon account.

- ✔ **Odd jobs.** Babysit. Pick up dog poop. Decorate someone's house for them for the holidays. Be an errand runner. Plant flowers and pull weeds. Wash cars. Mow lawns. Any job that needs to be done, do it. Take old ladies to the hair salon. Drive seniors to their medical appointments. Be a mom's helper and shuttle kids to after school activities. One never runs out of odd jobs.

✔ **Craigslist.** 40 million people are on craigslist. If you have something to sell, sell it. If you have a service to offer, offer it. The listing is free and it is the go-to place for online transactions. If you don't want to do a yard sale, every week post an item or two on craigslist and get rid of it all like that. No issues with rain on craigslist.

✔ **Parking space.** If you have a good spot in an urban area, rent it out. For example, if you take the train and have a parking pass, let someone know and your spot will go to the highest bidder. You can carpool or walk or bike to the station. If you live in an area where parking is a premium when events are going on, rent out your driveway and front yard to people needing a parking place.

✔ **Make stuff.** If you are crafty, go for it. You can sell anything online with sites like etsy or you can have your own simple web page. You can sell at local craft fairs, too.

✔ **Part-time job.** Never overlook the obvious. You can make nice money with a side gig. A part-time job often leads to full-time, and many employers offer benefits to part-time workers these days.

✔ **Home Based Business.** Anything goes. Whatever you love, whatever you are good at, put it to work for you. Help people with computers. Write resumes. Be a dog walker. Make money working from home. One couple started out helping friends by preparing hundreds of water balloons and now they have a thriving business selling and sending ready-to-go water balloons all across the country.

✔ **Be a delivery guy.** No joke. Print up free business cards at vistaprint.com or some other online service and make a flyer that you put in mailboxes in your community. Busy professionals and elderly are two great target markets. Call yourself Hometown Deliveries or even use the name of your town. San Diego Deliveries. Groceries. Dry Cleaning. Post Office Runs. Pharmacy Needs. Package/Courier Service. Restaurant Take Out.

Many people don't have time to do their errands and many senior citizens do not like to drive. Home based entrepreneurs always need someone to do their running for them, and be the lunch guy. People want to eat food from Freddy's Sandwich Shop, but Freddy doesn't deliver. Not smart on Freddy's part, but you can be bringer of lunch. That will earn you a nice tip, too.

You can take care of your personal business while you are building a business taking care of other's personal business. Call yourself a Life Saver. And, be sure to send in a thank you when your business like this takes off.

✔ **Go for the Gold**. Sell your jewelry. Gold is still commanding a nice price. Cash in old stuff you no longer like or wear. Give up Grandma's brooch, your wedding rings from your first marriage and the gold chain from the 80s. Cash looks so much better on you.

There are fifty ways to leave a lover and just as many to make fast money. Challenge yourself.

I know people who can make $10K in a day doing simple stuff that anyone, including you, can do. Need more idea starters?

✔ **eBay.** This classic is still simply the hands-down easy and surefire quick way to put some greenback in your wallet. eBay remains hugely popular because it works. You've got something to sell and there is somebody out there that wants to buy it.

Take a look around your house. Go through the garage. Spend an hour in the attic. What has been sitting in your basement for years that you forgot you even had? If you are a "normal" American, you hang on to stuff for the eternal "just in case I might need it someday." We end up with a lot of stuff that we never use. I know a guy who keeps everything, but then when he does need it, he can't find it. So he goes out and buys another one. He has two of just about everything. He could make a fortune selling his stuff.

Even if you are not a stockpiler or a hoarder or an unorganized "where did I put that?" kind of person like my friend, I can pretty much guarantee that you have stuff you can get rid of. We all do. If you can see that your stuff really is cash in your pocket, it makes it easier to part with.

Got golf clubs that you haven't used in three years? Get rid of them. Maybe a bike or roller blades? If you have kids, you have a never-ending turnover of stuff that you can get rid of when they outgrow it or tire of it. Famous brand children's clothing makes a killing on eBay. Their toys, your toys, your tools, the possibilities are endless.

The beauty of eBay is how easy it is and how easy it is for you to get paid. Set up a PayPal account (it's quick and easy and requires no technical savvy), and the payments you receive are deposited right into your PayPal account. You don't have to deal with credit cards or worrying if the buyer's check is going to bounce. You just sit back and watch the balance in your account go up, up, up.

You could make $10K in a day just from eBay.

✔ **craigslist**. The other great internet gold mine besides eBay is craigslist. There really is a guy named Craig who started an online version of a buy it/sell it bulletin board. Remember in college when people would post little notes by the campus mailbox? "Need a ride to San Diego this weekend." "Have a motorcycle to sell." "Looking for a roommate this summer?"

The concept is the same, but the venue has gone global. If you have something to offer, there is someone looking for it and they will look on craigslist. Go to www.craigslist.com and check it out. The possibilities are endless.

Sell your car, motorcycle, scooter, boat, Winnebago RV, your electronics, your jewelry, your collectibles. If you have a vacation home, rent it for a week and make big bucks fast.

If you live in New York or any other cool place that people want to visit, rent out your apartment for a week and get quick cash. It is amazing the transactions that can happen, if you use your creative mind. Think cash and think fast and it will be yours.

Sell your kittens, sell your kids (kidding). Peruse craigslist and it will give you ideas of what you are sitting on that could turn into fast money.

✔ **Sell your car**. Dude, seriously, sell your car.

You can use eBay or craigslist or any other online site. You can set it in front of your house with a For Sale sign. You can run an ad in your local paper. You can take it to a used car lot and see what they will give you. You can simply tell a friend to tell everyone he knows that you have a car for sale.

Word of mouth is often the best way to get things done and costs you nothing. If you live in a metropolitan area with good public transportation, you honestly do not need a car. When you need a car to do something you cannot do by walking, biking, public transportation, or carpooling, rent a car.

The money spent to rent a car on occasion is much less than the cost of car payments, insurance, and maintenance. And parking. If you have lived in a city, you know what a hassle parking can be.

Maybe you simply can't live without your car. Or you think you can't anyway. I suggest letting the idea gel for a while. Motor scooters are a great alternative transportation. And when you need to take a long road trip, borrow a buddy's wheels. Or call the rental guys.

✔ **Sell your toys.** If you have a boat, sell it. That equates to a large chunk of change immediately. Are you an avid boater? Do you live in a climate where you can use your boat most of the year?

If not, think about how much you spend on the watercraft and how much enjoyment you get out of it. If you are in a climate where you only have three months of boating weather and you are paying for storage the other nine months, selling your boat can be an instant cure and instant fast cash.

When you want to play on the water, go with a friend or rent a boat. You can rent a boat for an afternoon, a weekend, a week. It will be such a relief, you will wonder why you didn't do this sooner.

Same goes with jet skis, snow skis, kayaks, canoes, or any other kind of toy that you use once in a while for fun and most of the year it sits there costing you money. Sell it! Make money fast! You can rent the toys when you have a spare weekend for fun, and instead of the repairs, maintenance, storage and hassle, you will have spare change in your pocket now.

✔ **Sell your collections.** Most folks have something that they have been hanging on to for years and then they reach a point in their lives when their interests change, and those collections no longer mean anything to them. Are you a collector? Then there is cash to be had.

The baseball cards you have been collecting since you were a kid have value. If the sentimental value is no longer there for you, it's time to cash in. There are other collectors out there that want your stash, and there are buyers simply because there is money there. If you are knowledgeable, you can buy and sell and make a nice sum. You can sell off or you can be a trader.

I know of a guy who is a collector of old and rare coins. He makes great money selling to stores and other collectors. There are all kinds of collectibles out there. Stamps, postcards, antique toys, trinkets and glassware from different eras. If your passion is Depression glass or Victorian silver, there is a market.

Maybe you are not a collector now. If this area interests you as a way to make fast money, you can get up to speed on the value and availability of certain collectibles by researching on the internet and in magazines and other publications on that particular item and area of interest.

People make great money at flea markets and antique shows and estate sales. If you know about pot belly stoves or beaded jewelry or what have you, the money is there to be made. And, you can have a lot of fun in the process.

✔ **Consult**. Find consulting jobs that pay an advance. You can use your expertise to make a quick buck. People need what you know. What is your area of expertise? Find a consulting job by word of mouth or online at www.csc.com, www.careerbuilder.com, and ops-jobs.theladders.com/Management-Consulting.

✔ **Craft, Cook, Cater…**Are you starting to see all the possibilities? You can make baby blankies, booties and bonnets. People are always having babies. You can cook meals for parties or for busy people. You can cater events, parties, functions. Maybe you make cupcakes. Maybe you do the whole thing. You know how to do stuff. Make fast money from it!

✔ **Audition**. Audition for modeling opportunities. There are legitimate needs for print and video ads. Television commercials need local people. Flyers for ads too. Maybe you can audition for acting parts as well. You can make money!

✔ **Licensing**. Are you an idea person? Inventing cool stuff all the time? Finding ways to do stuff better? License your product or idea to an infomercial company. Infomercial companies are often willing to see you on short notice and move aggressively, if they like your product. Many are willing to pay $10–30,000 just for licensing plus a royalty. That is FAT fast money!

✔ **Use your house**. Live in a town where things happen? Super Bowl, Final Four, Olympics? Rose Parade? Glee tour? Have a condo somewhere lovely? Rent out your house. People will pay huge money!

✔ **Think timely**. While I am on the subject of big events, sell time sensitive items when the time is hot and you can make outrageous sums of money. Sell Super Bowl champion shirts the week of the big game. Sell the big concert shirts. People made money off the End of The World event of 12/21/12. There will always be something. Use that brain and your purse will thank you.

✔ **Assignment of contract.** Want to make a large sum of cash in an amazingly short amount of time? And, want to do so with no risk? I thought you might be interested. Well, there is a slight risk involved. One dollar.

An ideal way to turn a quick deal and make thousands of dollars, this strategy is certainly one of my favorites. The possibilities are endless and the sky is the limit when it comes to how much you can make.

Call yourself the middleman in this scenario, the money-man. Basically, an assignment of contract is a transaction between a person who has something to sell and you, except that you do not want the asset that the person is selling. You want money.

So you make a deal with the seller. You agree to enter into a contract to purchase the thing that he is selling. You put up $1.00 in order to make the contract legally binding and you agree to buy the asset for a certain price in a certain period of time, and—here is the important part—you have an assignment clause in the contract. That means you can assign to someone else your right to buy this asset. You don't want it, whatever the "it" is; you want to make some cash on the deal. Basically, you tie up the asset for one dollar, and have the "option" to pay the balance at a given time in the future (e.g., within 30, 60, or 90 days).

You have a buyer who wants the asset, or you find one. You assign the contract to this person for a price greater than your contract with the seller and you keep the difference. For example: Bob has a house that has a value of $100,000 that he needs to sell. You contract with Bob for $1 that you will buy the house for $60,000 and your agreement states that you can assign the contract to someone else. You agree that you (or your assignee) will buy the house within 60 days or you forfeit your dollar. You then assign the contract to a buyer that you found who is willing to buy the house for $90,000. You get to keep the difference. $30,000! That is a nice return on a one-dollar investment!

This method can be done with real estate, cars, jewelry, furniture, artwork, etc., etc., etc. The possibilities are endless! You find someone with something to sell. You find someone who wants to buy it. You are the match maker, money maker.

If you know the deal ahead of time, you know the seller and his item and you know you have a buyer, you can hook them up and you get a finder's fee. You can make a nice commission this way, too. It's all timing.

If you do not have a buyer in hand, and you know you can get one within the 90 days of the contract, you do the assignment of contract thing. Make sense? You can be a wheeler dealer and make a lot of fast money this way.

✔ **Get a loan**. That seems like a no-brainer, so we sometimes overlook the obvious. Need money fast? Get a loan from a local guy or check out the online lenders. If you need money in a pinch, go after it. ASK. Would you be willing...Use the strategies you have learned already and put them to good use.

There are many sources of loans. Think logical and think outside the box.

o **Take a loan against your 401(k).** If you have a nice nest egg in the retirement account and want money right here, right now, tap into the money sitting there. You get it quick, you get a good interest rate, and you are paying yourself back, not a bank.

o **Take a loan against other investment accounts.** Same logic applies here as well. Quick, liquid cash available when you need it. Pay back yourself at a good rate.

o **Cash advance on your credit card.** If you need money now, take advantage of the credit card in your wallet. You can get immediate cash in the blink of an eye.

o **Phone a friend.** Maybe you have a friend or relative who owes you money. Now is the time to collect. Or maybe you have a friend or relative who always offers you a loan. If you want quick cash in a jiffy, accept the loan with heartfelt thanks. Maybe they will even give it to you interest free.

o **Get an advance from your employer.** Depending upon your type of work and the method of payment, you may be able to get an advance from your employer. If you know you have a good commission check coming next month, take it as an advance now, if you need the funds pronto.

o **Equity line.** If you are a homeowner, access your home equity line of credit. You can get big sums, pay little interest, and have the cash in hand with the snap of a finger.

Do you see how many sources there are for money that we forget about?

I have written many books, including other informational books to keep you in good financial shape. Have you read any of my Free Money material?

When we did the first *Debt Cures* book, I started to learn about all the free money and funding that is available. Coupons and free stuff. Government grants from state, local, and federal agencies. Private foundations offer money. Corporations have programs where they give free money.

> ...extra money is always a worthwhile venture.

Free money

Tons of resources and information. Most people think you have to be poor or part of some sort of demographic to qualify. Nope. There are grants for everyone and free money from other sources, too.

Grants are great—money from the government that you never have to pay back! It's not just grants. There are also ways to find free money and "lost" money.

Another way to some fast money is lost money. Or, should I say found money?! There are thousands upon thousands of dollars that literally could have your name on it. You are entitled to what is yours! Maybe it is old savings bonds that you forgot about, or an old bank account, or pension account. There are many sources of "forgotten" money and that money is just sitting waiting to be claimed.

There is $16.5 billion in unclaimed savings bonds alone. When these savings bonds were sold, the Bureau of the Public Debt collected the name and address of the bond owner. This contact information is literally buried within five billion microfilm issuance records. The vast majority of microfilm records are not indexed and difficult to access. As a result, no one is actively searching for the owners of these matured, unredeemed savings bonds.

The federal government does not have an active program or practical set of procedures to locate these bondholders to reunite them with the proceeds of their investment.

You can do the search. You just might be surprised. Lots of people find that they have saving bonds and all kinds of other money too, that they forgot about or didn't even really know about.

Go to unclaimedasssets.com and find out if you are among the missing. Try missingmoney.com too, and unclaimed.org too.

Missingmoney.com is a national, searchable database endorsed by NAUPA and all the participating state unclaimed property offices.

Unclaimed assets

NAUPA is the National Association of Unclaimed Property Administrators is affiliated with the National Association of State Treasurers. States are the keepers of unclaimed assets. Individuals conduct millions of searches every year and millions of claims are filed every year to collect that money. You've got nothing to lose. Searching is always free.

These web sites are veritable goldmines. There are many places holding unclaimed assets and some of those assets may find their way back to you.

Besides lost United States savings bonds, there are bank accounts, pension accounts, social security checks, veterans' benefits, life insurance, tax refunds, and the list goes on and on. There are store refunds and rebates and utility deposits waiting to be claimed. There are BILLIONS of dollars and MILLIONS of people who need to find each other!

Most of these web links require just a name and social security number to do the check for you. It's so quick and so easy. I even found money coming to me that I didn't know about. I have a very wealthy friend who found lost money in his name, too. Income doesn't matter if you are rich—if it is yours, it's yours! Claim it!

For more FREE MONEY sources, get my other book, Kevin Trudeau's *Free Money They Don't Want You to Know About!* What I share here is just a tiny sampling of what I share in that book.

Don't forget about that money source called old tax refunds. It could be possible that Uncle Sam didn't find you and you have some refunds from years past that never found their way to you.

There is over a BILLION bucks in unclaimed tax refunds. Maybe some of that is yours. To find out, simply go online to www. irs.gov and click on "Where's my refund." To research the missing refund, you need to know your social security number, your filing status (married filing joint, single, married filing separate, head of household, or qualifying widow/er), and the dollar amount of the refund you are expecting. (FYI—Always keep a copy of your tax returns!)

If you don't have all this information, contact the feds with what you do have and ask where your money is. One reader, Veronica, received over $28,000. That's worth a little effort on your part, wouldn't you say?

The IRS folks will look into your situation and see what happened to your money. Many times it is because they cannot deliver your check. The IRS does not allow mail to be forwarded. If this is the problem with your account, you can go online to update your current address. Every year, at least 25,000 pieces of mail do not get delivered.

> There are many places holding unclaimed assets...

If you have an IRS taxpayer service office in your town, you can walk in with proof of ID and ask them to look up your past years to make sure there is no unpaid money sitting in their coffers that should be in your pockets.

Samples

I have included a sampling for you so you can get an idea of all the free money possibilities. Also see the Free Money chapter near the end of this book.

For example, it can be as easy as free coupons and free samples. Check out fatwallet.com, couponchief.com, coolsavings.com, Pricegrabber.com, and smartaboutmoney.org.

There are many private foundations that give free money as well. Sometimes you have to fill out an application. Sometimes you don't.

This is just a taste. There are unlimited ways to fast money to help you get out of debt and to help you build your wealth.

Are the wheels turning? Are you thinking? Get your creative juices flowing and start thinking of ways in your life that you can make money fast.

Any one of these ways could net you ten grand. How much fast money do you want to make?

Seriously. Be creative. Be bold. Think about starting a business.

I know someone who makes and sells decorated cakes and makes great money at it. Same for another friend who makes specialty cookies. I also know someone who is a personal chef for others and makes nice money.

I just read a story of a hairdresser who got laid off. Yeah, every industry is hurting and no one is exempt from the pink slip. This gal didn't just go cry and pout. She heard from a friend that the elderly population cannot get out to the beauty salon, but want their hair done. This laid-off lady took her scissors and shampoo and started making house calls.

She found a whole new business opportunity and makes even more money than she did when she was a regular stylist at the mall. Just because you keep hearing "times are tough" does not mean that opportunity does not exist.

Start small

Every success story started as a small story. Mrs. Fields' Cookies, the Auntie Em Pretzels, every ice cream or juice guy or whatever. They started out of necessity or just for fun, and the business exploded into a full-blown big deal.

I know a gal who makes bowls and purses out of old vinyl record albums. I know a guy who makes lamps out of wine bottles. I know a husband and wife team who started a business helping other parents navigate the waters of college aid and scholarships.

Think about the products that you know and love. You can sell them and make money. If you use a product and love it, don't you want to tell other people about it? And, if you can help them out by offering the benefits of such product, wouldn't you want to do that? And, if you make money along the way in doing so, even better.

Pick a product that you are passionate about it. Passion sells. The product you choose to sell should be something you believe in and something that is consumable. That means your customers will run out of it and need to order more.

Face cream. Nutrition supplements. Whatever. What do you love that you want to be a distributor of? You can start with anything.

I know a guy who sells candles and does okay, and yes, candles technically run out. But people buy them more as a favor to him or as a fundraiser kind of thing for their kids' school, not because they need another smelly candle.

That can be how you get started. Whatever your product is, let it be your Product Wow. Something that wows you and will wow others.

Little by little, they started telling their friends and family about "Product Wow." And little by little, more people tried it and liked it too. They started selling Product Wow to said friends and family. The next thing they knew, they had a little side business and money was coming in, and it was all quite effortless.

The money became a wow factor too.

So then, the realization comes over them and they decide to put a little more time into this side business and it really takes off.

Sitting at home on the computer or talking on the phone to friends and acquaintances, a business is born.

Once you get your customers rolling, they usually can order from you or online. They can refer other customers to you or become distributors themselves and you get a reward for being the one to introduce to them to the company. You sit back and get nice monthly checks for doing nothing more than telling people about a product that you believe in.

Passion

It all starts with passion about a product and when it is a consumable product, the sky is the limit where profits are involved. Selling objects can be great, but it is not the same thing. A great lamp is a great lamp, but if it can last a lifetime, there are no repeat sales. The idea of these companies is repeat business.

If the vitamin drink you enjoy every morning is nearing empty, you order more. So you want to get involved with a product that is something that gets used up. I know people who make great incomes by selling nutritional supplements, skin care items, make up and beauty products, and even greeting cards through an online distributor system.

The real treat is that you keep making money long after the initial sale. The residual income that comes to you month after month is the golden nugget. Spend a little bit of time getting people interested, then you make the sale and then you do nothing and you keep making money.

Think about the products that you love and use regularly. Become a distributor and turn on everyone you know to why you love it. Then tell everyone you meet. You can be sitting next to someone on an airplane and in the normal chit chat of conversation that takes place, you can make a new customer. That new customer might become a distributor too. The income potential is off the charts.

It's easy. It's fun. It's usually no inventory and very little up-front costs to you to get started. People order and get their stuff shipped directly to them. You can have customers all over the country and depending upon the product, all over the world.

> Become a distributor and turn on everyone you know to why you love it.

Forming a company has many benefits. You can get more credit as a business owner than as an individual. Your credit scores are separate, you the individual and you the business.

Not that hard

It is easier than you think to form a business. You can form an LLC online at www.legalzoom.com. It's fast and simple and not expensive.

Another great bonus is that as a business, you have access to a much larger line of credit. MUCH LARGER. You could qualify for a line of credit of a million bucks. The great thing about a line of credit is that it is there for you, ready and waiting. You use a little of it or a lot of it, you make the decision. It is not a loan with a set installment payment. It is a pot of gold waiting for you at the end of your rainbow.

In general, the interest rates are usually lower for corporate businesses too. With your corporate tax ID number, you are a separate entity with a whole new fresh credit record. It's a bold new landscape.

Yet another huge benefit to forming your own company is the tax breaks you get. You can deduct all your business expenses and these can be quite substantial. When you are a business owner, much of what you spend time on and spend money on is for your business. Those expenses can be written off!

Talk to your financial advisor about forming a corporation or LLC and get started today.

Let me know what works for you and what you did that is not listed here. Your ideas could be printed in a future issue of our *Debt Cures* newsletter.

CHAPTER 14

The New Economy

"In the old industrial economy, the best client was one who could pay off debts. In the post-industrial economy, the best customer is the person who can't pay it off."
—Robert Manning,
director consumer financial center

Somewhere along the way, the credit card industry lost sight of being a service and convenience for its customers. It became cutthroat and greedy. With the change in our economy, the abusive practices have only gotten worse.

Over the years, the banks and credit card companies have devised more and more devious ways to get money out of the innocent credit card user. Racking up the interest rate and devising more fees. Allowing charges that put the cardholder over his limit and then charging him a fee for going over. Charging a fee when a customer is given the convenience of paying her bill over the phone.

The new regulations that came down did not do any good to the American citizen. It is business as usual. Credit card companies now have to include notice before changing terms such as interest rates, but you are stuck with them unless you can pay the whole balance off and be done with them. Or maybe you can find a balance transfer option.

The credit card creeps now have to put on your statement how long it will take you to pay off that balance, if all you do is pay the minimum amount due. It does not change the fact that it will still take you ten years to pay off a five hundred dollar balance, if all you pay is the minimum payment of $17. Ten years!

Review statements

Read your statements, people! I hold a Macy's American Express statement in my hands. Balance of $510.86 with a minimum payment of $17 due. If that is all I pay and never use this card again, I will take ten years to pay off that five hundred bucks and eighty-six cents. PLUS I will have paid $914 in interest.

Nine hundred bucks more they get out of you, if you pay just the minimum monthly payment. Do you see how they are not doing you any favors?!

Some folks think it is grand to have such a dinky amount to pay each month. Oh gee, isn't that nice. Sure, for the credit card folks. An extra nine hundred bucks for them is just peachy.

That card had a high APR of 18.74%. Do you know what interest rates you have on all your cards? Do you know what balances you have on all your credit cards? If not, stop right now. Get out all your statements. Get a pen. Get a piece of paper. Column one, name of credit card. Column two, amount you owe. Column three, credit limit. Column four, minimum payment. Column five, interest rate APR. Column six, how many years it would take if all you paid was the minimum monthly payment. Column seven, the interest you would pay.

Total up the amount you owe.

Total up the interest you would owe.

Make you sick?

Use this piece of paper as your plan of attack. If you have a 0% or low interest card, switch high interest balances over there.

Plan of attack

Make more than the monthly minimum payment. Create a plan of what balance to pay and congratulate yourself when you get a card paid off. Make efforts to cut back on using those cards.

When you see where the money is going, and it's not for your benefit, it makes it easier to find ways to use cash instead of the credit card. If you think you cannot come up with cash, please refer back to the Fast Money chapter.

If you want to continue paying for bankers and creditors to take vacations and buy luxury yachts, then just keep on with what you've been doing.

Yeah, I thought so.

Pay attention to your credit cards. That is the bottom line. The regulations may change in order to "protect" you, and the credit card creeps will keep coming up with ways to "abuse" you. The best protection for you is your knowledge bank.

Every time the government does something to reign in one kind of fee that the banks and credit industry charge, the banks and credit industry fight back. Who loses in this fight? The consumer, of course.

Fees keep coming, fast and furious. Right now about 10% of the population pays at least ten bucks a month in bank fees, and that's just overdraft fees. Ten percent of the people with bank accounts pay every month due to overdraft.

The average overdraft fee is over $30. If you write a check or use your debit card with insufficient funds, ch-ching.

Sometimes people do not know when the account is low. We pay with check, debit card an online bill pay. It's not always clear what the account balance is at any given time.

"Protection"

You can opt out of "protection" at your bank with your debit card. If you do so, your purchase on your debit card would be declined. You would know at the checkout line that you don't have enough funds. You would have to find another way to make the purchase (or not make it) and you would avoid a thirty dollar overdraft fee.

If you currently allow your bank to process the debit card transaction, even if you do not have enough money, you can change this option. You can opt out and they no longer will be able to charge you the fee.

With checks, we're out of luck. When you send a check, you think there is money in the bank to cover it. By the time the other party cashes it, your account situation has changed and the check bounces. There is nothing you can do. You are dinged with a fee.

It can get crazy. Some banks allow four overdraft fees per day. At $35 a pop, that tallies up to $140 a day. They can do it for several days, if you stay in the hole. That adds up to $700 in just five days.

And then they can add on an EXTENDED overdraft penalty fee. As if the $700 wasn't penalty enough.

One study shows the national average in overdraft fees is just over $1,000. Understand that a national average means there were higher figures than that in the calculation.

The best strategy is to opt out of the bank's overdraft coverage. They want you to overdraw so they can apply fees.

Sign up for e-mail and text alerts to notify you when you are low in funds.

Monitor your account and know your balance. Sign up for e-mail and text alerts to notify you when you are low in funds. Use direct deposit. It gets your money in quicker and you can avoid fees by using direct deposit and perhaps the bank will offer a free checking account.

You can link your savings account to your checking account. In the event your checking gets low, an automatic transfer from savings will cover the deficit. There is usually a fee, but it's less than the overdraft fee. Ten bucks is better than $35.

The new laws require that you opt in for that overdraft "protection." The new law did not say that fees would go away. Fees have indeed gone up.

When President Obama made a Rose Garden ceremony out of the signing of the new law, he stated that credit card companies have "made it difficult" for folks who carry a balance on their accounts and are trying to get out of debt.

Made it difficult.

And they say this guy is eloquent?

The Prez said that many people got trapped when the economy tanked. How true. He also made it clear that the disaster is due to the practices of the credit card industry.

Millions in debt

That was during his first administration that the new credit card regulations were passed. Here we are, standing in a bed of thorns. Millions of folks are still over their heads in credit card debt.

People are out of work. People are out of their homes. Slapping the wrists of the credit industry didn't do a darn thing.

The lenders want people who cannot pay off their bills. They want customers for life. They want you to pay that minimum payment every month.

Elizabeth Warren, a Harvard Law School professor, who we quoted in the first *Debt Cures* book for her work on the PBS documentary "The Secret History of Credit Cards," was featured in the Los Angeles Times: "Research conducted by a team including Elizabeth Warren, a Harvard Law School professor and consumer debt expert, suggests that people who fall into serious debt tend to do so because of a harsh roll of the dice—job loss, illness, divorce—and not profligate spending."

Folks are not spending themselves into this hell hole. They are simply trying to live, to get by.

Elizabeth Warren has become even more passionate about the credit world since that PBS expose. After the 2012 election, an article from Reuters stated: Consumer financial advocates and bankers focused on the Senate run of Elizabeth Warren, the consumerist who dreamed up the Consumer Financial Protection Bureau and helped establish it. She is already talking about being the Senate's primary watchdog on such issues as banking disclosures and student loans.

In a speech during her Senate run, she stated that she never dreamed she would run for the Senate. She also said: "I talk to nurses and programmers, salespeople and firefighters—people who bust their tails every day. Not one of them—not one—stashes their money in the Cayman Islands to avoid paying their fair share of taxes."

I have a hunch you are busting your tail and do not have money stashed in any offshore accounts.

Fighting abuse

Warren's passion for fighting the abuse of the credit industry is what got our attention several years ago. One internet report on her Senate run stated: "Warren spoke on the impact on middle-class Americans of rising health-care costs, burgeoning debt, and the depletion of not only their savings, but also with the rise in joblessness, their confidence. She spoke of "the Wild West" conditions deregulation had created, where banks could sell virtually any product they wanted, on any terms: mortgages they knew consumers could not pay off, credit cards whose rates they could raise at whim."

Look back at my previous *Debt Cures* books. I compared the banking and credit industry to the Wild West and things have not changed much. They are still outlaws who think they are above the law.

Warren still talks about harsher rules for the credit agencies: "The rules are the same. Nothing has changed. The laws have not changed. They continue to run their credit rating agencies in the way they believe will best enhance their own profits and revenues. You have to change the rules of the road."

We'll see how the road goes.

> The rules are the same. Nothing has changed.

Warren stated: "We can make the system work with regulation. I'm not somebody who believes it's time to throw the whole thing out. But regulation has got to support it. And the way it supports it is it increases transparency in this system, it increases honesty in the system. It increases accountability in the system. When you get those things there's plenty of room to make profits. There's plenty of room to be rich, I'm all for that. But it's got to be profits that were made honestly."

That's where the banks and credit creeps have a hard time. She touts some of what we tout. We're all for making money. Everyone can and should make money. It's the abuse that needs to go.

Predatory lenders

During Warren's stint at the CFPB, she made it the bureau's mission to protect consumers from predatory lenders. She was the driving force who birthed the idea for a government agency that would protect consumers from tricks and traps perpetrated by banks, mortgage firms, and credit card companies.

The Consumer Financial Protection Bureau mission is to "make markets for consumer financial products and services work for Americans—whether they are applying for a mortgage, choosing among credit cards, or using any number of other consumer financial products."

Warren is back at Harvard and the CFPB marches on in its efforts to protect American consumers from the clutches of the evil doings of the credit lending institutions. You do not have to take abuse and you have every right to consumer financial products that work to your benefit. No more do we sit back and think the big guys have all the power.

The more you know, the stronger you are. It's good to be in the know. Keep on.

CHAPTER 15

The New Way to Play

"Get up, stand up, stand up for your rights."
—Bob Marley

Now you know your rights. You have the right to be treated with respect. You have the right to not pay stupid fees because the whining banks aren't making enough money. You have the right to know what goes on with your credit card billing.

You have the right to make decisions based on the truth, not fear.

So do your homework. Keep up to date with the latest news and one great way to do that is the *Debt Cures* monthly newsletter. We bring you information to help you every step of the way.

Be smart. Don't get lazy and don't start trusting your bank or credit card company. They are not looking out for your best interests. It should be obvious to you by now that they are only concerned with their interests.

So, use all the ways you can to keep tabs on your account balance: online, at an ATM machine, and over the phone. Use an "alert" system via text or e-mail to be notified when your balance is getting low.

Stay on top of your accounts. Just like it is up to you to monitor your credit score and credit report and be vigilant there, it is up to you to be vigilant in your bank records. They want to lull you into complacency. They want to catch you napping so they can slap you with fees. Fees. Fees. Fees. That is their bread and butter, never forget it.

The fee racket is just that and it is huge money. That is why the banks do it, of course. They are looking for new ways all the time to put the squeeze on the American citizen.

Be responsible for you

The Center for Responsible Lending keeps their eye on what is going on. The fees are out of whack. A few years ago they reported that the amount of actual overdraws is $15 billion. The bank loves it because they make even more on it. For that $15 billion, their take is more than $17.5 billion. They make billions and billions of dollars in this one fee area alone.

Have you ever had an overdraft? Most people have. Let's say the bank cleared a check and you went ten bucks in the hole. For that measly ten bucks, they charge you $39 for it! Gimme a break!

The FDIC states that most overdrafts are small amounts.

Not many people know their balance down the penny all the time and we forget checks we write and debit card purchases made. We think we have money in the account and when we cut it close, we overdraw, usually not by much.

The bankers rub their hands in glee. They now get to add to their billions for that oversight. So, be diligent. Monitor your accounts and get the alerts. Every time you overdraw, you are allowing them to turn the knife in our collective wounds.

Shop for a bank with the lowest fees and use an online bank, a local credit union or community bank. They usually have lower fees.

If you are shopping for a credit card, be a sleuth and get what you want. Do not pay all those fees. Do not agree to a high interest rate. Don't fall for a low teaser introductory rate, if the regular rate after that time period is up is going to be crazy high. Make sure that balance transfer fees do not apply or are reasonable.

Ask

Now you know to ask about all that. Pretty simple.

At the risk of sounding like a broken record, be diligent in your efforts to get the best rate. If you sign up for the intro teaser rate and they will only give you a card with a different rate because your credit is not so great, say no thanks.

Now you know to pay attention to all that. Pretty simple.

If the intro rate is great, but the balance transfer fee is high, think first. Get out the calculator and ballpark the numbers. Maybe to transfer $5,000 to a new card will cost you $200. What interest are you paying on that card? How soon can you pay it off? Crunch your figures before you go leaping.

Now you know to take a second look. Pretty simple.

Credit cards always used to offer a 30-day grace period. That means you had thirty days to pay the balance before any interest accrued. Now, the grace period is much less, usually twenty days, and some cards don't give you any. Find out before you sign up for a card. If there is no grace period, you don't really want that card.

Now you know what to be on the lookout for. Pretty simple.

To search for the right card for you, use the internet. Some sites are better than others. I do not get a kickback for naming any, but I will suggest www.cardratings.com and www.creditcards.com. They offer updated information and articles and news you can use about what is going on in the credit card industry.

Free resources

Use these comprehensive free sources. You can compare over 500 different credit cards. You can read over 20,000 reviews so you know what others have experienced and what advice they have to give.

> You can find offers if you have no credit.

Another source I can recommend to you, especially if you are trying to get a credit card while you are in the process of improving your credit score, is www.credit.com. Take a peek at http://www.credit.com/credit-cards/bad-credit/. This section features credit cards for people with bad credit.

There are credit cards and prepaid cards for those of you who are struggling and want to get back or create good credit. Where there is a will, there's a way, and a credit card.

You can also search for the best card depending upon where you fall in the credit score numbers. One site does the breakdown as:

Excellent = 750+
Good = 700–749
Fair = 650–699
Poor = 600–649
Bad = Below 599

You can even find offers if you have no credit. It is worthwhile to know your credit score and know where that places you in the credit world. The better the score, the better card deal you are able to get.

These sites give their top picks and provide the contact info if you want to apply for any of the cards. You can start the process with a simple click.

Another site for those who need a card and have credit trouble. Go to www.newhorizon.org/Info/unsecured.htm.

At newhorizon.org, they list unsecured credit cards for people with bad credit. These cards do not require money down like secured cards. Sometimes with bad credit, the idea is to reestablish credit, so you put down a deposit and receive a card in that amount.

These cards at this site are unsecured, like a "normal" credit card. So even if you have bad credit, you can get a card with no money down. These cards report to the credit reporting agencies and that is how you work your way back to good credit. Make regular monthly on-time payments. Each month that gets generated into the credit report.

Be aware that you may have to pay a fee for this process.

What you can buy

There are alternatives now out there that you can buy at places like WalMart. American Express has something called Bluebird, a checking and debit alternative from American Express. They call it loaded with features, not fees.

You buy the little blue box at the checkout. It is a starter kit. It comes with a Starter Card. You deposit money on it right there at the cash register check out. You can then begin using your card right away. You can go online to access all of the Bluebird features.

The Bluebird card allows ATM access with no surcharges at select ATMs. There is no activation fee. There is no annual fee or monthly fee. There is no overdraft fee. There is no minimum balance requirement. There is no credit inquiry to affect your credit score.

With your Bluebird card, you can make deposits, make purchases, pay bills, withdraw money, make accounts for family members, and make transfers to other Bluebird accounts. To make deposits into your Bluebird account, you can set up direct deposit from your paycheck, transfer money from a bank account, deposit checks using the Bluebird mobile app, or add cash directly to the account at WalMart or with cash reload packs that you can pay at some stores.

You can use the card to make purchases like you would any other American Express card. There are no foreign exchange fees if you make purchases while traveling out of the country. You can pay bills with your Bluebird account online or with the mobile app.

If your friends have Bluebird accounts, you can transfer money to their accounts to pay them back for when they picked up the tab for dinner or whatever. You can track and manage your spending at Bluebird.com. You get fraud protection and customer service through American Express. The funds you put on the card do not expire. Once you load the starter card, you go online to Bluebird. com to register and get full benefits.

There are always ways to get what you need. Unlike Mick Jagger and the Rolling Stones, I think you often can get what you want too.

Common sense

Much of what I preach and teach is common sense. I will assume that you have credit card debt on several credit cards. Most Americans have thousands in debt and have many cards in use. I will also assume that you want to pay it off as quickly as possible.

The accelerated payment method does exactly that. Take a look at all your credit card balances and the interest rates. Pick the account that has the highest interest rate and concentrate on getting that card paid off. You are accelerating hard on that account. Your pedal is to the metal and your destination is a paid off card.

Keep making at least the minimum payment on all your other cards, but this one is your targeted attack. Make big chunks of payment on it every month. Because it has the highest rate, it is the one that is costing you the most. The longer you carry a balance, the more wasted dough on interest charges.

Use ways to make fast money and pay down the high interest card. When this account balance gets paid off, celebrate! The relief and sense of accomplishment that you will feel is great.

It gives you the confidence to tackle the next account with the next highest interest rate. *Debt Cures* is about giving you the confidence to take control of your financial situation. This accelerated repayment method is simply focusing on one account balance with more laser focus and more cash to get it off your plate.

Encouragement

For some people, they need quicker results to bring about that sense of achievement and give them the encouragement to keep marching on. For them, it is often suggested to pick the lowest credit card balance, no matter what the interest rates are on others. Pick the one that you can pay off quickly and do it. Pay it off.

The very reality of having it gone does wonders for the self-esteem. One less bill to pay next month is very freeing. It removes the burden and makes the whole get-out-of-debt concept seem possible.

> One less bill to pay next month is very freeing.

Some of you have been living with debt for so long that you can't imagine a different reality. That is why this method helps. It changes your reality in a tangible way. One less check to write this month, having that balance PAID IN FULL is freeing, and can spur you on to greater financial heights.

Depending upon your situation, one option to knocking off those pesky credit card bills overnight is to tap into your house. That could mean you use your home equity line and pay off the high interest credit card accounts.

This is not a fail-safe method. You need to be able to make the mortgage payment and the home equity repayment, but the equity line most often has a much better interest rate than any credit card. And, you are paying yourself back. If you are not planning on staying in your house for a while, this may not make sense for you. So, only you know what is right for you.

If you are having a tough time with making your bills, always pick up the phone and do what we have talked about. Explain your situation and how you want to make this debt go away. Explain that you want to pay, but you need them to meet you in the middle. Explain that you are trying to avoid bankruptcy and that if you went that route, they would not get paid at all.

They want some money. You want to pay some money. You can't pay it all right now. That's the cold hard truth. Talk to them about all the interest and penalty charges that have been racked up. Negotiate paying the principle balance and having the creditor wipe away the other fees.

Negotiate whatever you want, however you want. Different tactics work for different people, and every situation is different. Maybe you are Nice Guy and don't have it in you to raise your voice. Maybe you are Hard Ball Negotiator and have no qualms taking on the big dogs.

In this time and this economy, you've got nothing to lose and everything to gain. Ask and you shall receive. Demand. You will never know until you pick up the phone.

Clean off the bad marks

Don't forget to have your creditors wipe off any negative items from your credit report as well. They can do that. They can eliminate collection activity, so be sure to throw that request into your talks, too.

Imagine having the debt gone and the "bad marks" off your credit report. Your improved credit score will impact your life. Instead of feeling the negative, it can all be positive. The weight can be lifted off your shoulders. All you need to do is negotiate it.

One *Debt Cures* follower applied the simple art of negotiation and his debt went from topping out at around $50,000 all the way down to $13,000. He is among many *Debt Cures* success stories.

Another tool, tip, technique for your toolbox is to show the lenders that your net worth is not that of a multi-millionaire and that you simply cannot pay. Sometimes they simply need to see it in black and white that you simply cannot pay. This can make your debt go away.

To show lenders that they need to work with you to negotiate down the balance of your bills, you need to show your situation. Your current net worth can show that you have no more resources to pay what they are asking of you.

Take your personal financial statements to the bank or lender or collector: "You can squeeze all you want, but the well is dry. You can't get something that doesn't exist and my means to pay does not exist."

When they see that you are tapped out, so to speak, they usually are more willing to make a quick negotiation.

Show the numbers

A simple balance sheet and income statement are easy enough to do on your own. You can also hire a local accountant or if you have a friend who is an accountant or lawyer, they can draft a letter for you on their letterhead that simply states you have no ability to pay. With such a letter, the creditors are more willing to negotiate with you. They would rather get a little something than nothing at all.

The debt collector will see your financial statements and read your letter, which states very plainly: This is my net worth, consisting of these assets—my house, my cars, and my wedding rings; these liabilities: mortgage loan debt, car loan debt, credit card debt #1, credit card debt #2, student loan debt, etc.

A simple statement in black and white speaks volumes. After looking at this, your creditors should be more accessible and more realistic in their demands. For example, they won't keep insisting that you pay the whole $80,000 that you owe if it is clear that all you could ever pay is $10,000. And, maybe all you can pay is nothing. If you have a negative net worth, show it.

Money talks. And, no money may make them walk.

Money talks

The same thought principle applies to you and who you give your business to, right? Money talks. If they don't have any money perks for you, then it is up to you to walk.

For example, when you are shopping for a credit card, you have a lot of choices. Use the power that comes with choice. Don't be a patsy. Don't be a pushover. Start your power with choosing a credit card from the get-go.

There are lots of secrets perks that come with credit cards. See if yours have any of these benefits.

Most cards offer purchase protection. That means, if you buy something and it breaks or is stolen within the first 90 days, the credit card company writes you a check. That's right. Your purchases are protected—up to $1,000!

Many people are not aware of this perk. It's a great benefit that comes with many credit cards. Check your terms of agreement or call customer service to find out if your card offers this wonderful benny.

I read a blogger who spilled coffee on his new laptop. He submitted a claim to his credit card who wrote him a check. This guy, no dummy, then sold the computer on eBay for parts and got another six hundred bucks on top of that! Now he could go buy a new laptop and, of course, be smart to not spill his coffee again.

Hang on to your receipts for the first 90 days after a purchase in case you need to cash in on this benefit.

Take the perks

Many cards also offer price protection. If you buy something with your credit card and then the same item is advertised elsewhere for less, you can get the difference back. Usually these deals require that you have the print ad showing the exact item at a lower price than you paid and it must be within 60 days (sometimes less) of your purchase. Most cards that do this will refund the difference up to $250. Not everything under the sun is included, like most internet purchases, but for your store purchases, again, hang on to your receipts. If you see your purchased item advertised somewhere for less, you may get the overage you paid sent to you from your credit card company.

> You want the card that treats you the best.

Another perk that many cards offer is extended warranty coverage on your purchases. Your credit card will match whatever store/manufacturer warranty your new product comes with—up to one year. So, if you buy a new electronic gadget and it comes with a 1-year warranty, your credit card will provide an additional one-year warranty.

So, if in year two, your item breaks, just let your credit card company know and they'll reimburse you for repair or a new one.

Many credit cards also give perks when it comes to shopping for things like flowers, movie tickets, and at certain big name retailers. They cut deals with all these places and that gives you a discount when you use your card on these items. Read the promotional flyers that they send with your credit card agreement to see if they offer any discounts. Call customer service and ask who their promotional partners are and use them when shopping. Why not save a few more bucks whenever you can!

Most credit cards now offer a 24-hour personal concierge service, which will make your dinner reservations, purchase tickets to events, and almost anything else you can think of. If you are trying to snag concert tickets or sporting event tickets, call the credit card concierge and let them go to work trying to get those tickets. There is no guarantee, but it saves you a lot of time and often you score.

Many of you know this, but a reminder is always good. When you are renting a car, you don't have to go with their rental insurance. Your credit card usually provides up to $50,000 in secondary coverage for collision and theft. You have to book the rental car with your credit card, of course. Always make sure your card has the coverage. Many homeowners and auto insurance policies provide protection for rental cars as well.

Most credit cards provide free roadside assistance, so you can skip purchasing it for your car or when renting cars.

Credit cards have a lot of these protection benefits. Take advantage of them. Call your credit card company and have them send you a booklet of benefits so you know what you get with your card.

Use the perks that are out there. You have choices. If your current card does not offer you any of this stuff, keep that in mind when you are shopping and comparing for a new card company.

You want the card that treats you the best. These benefits alone add up to over a thousand bucks of benefit for you. Use it.

Credit cards aren't going away. Admit it, you use them. You might as well arm yourself with all the knowledge and power that you can. You might as well use them for every dime that you can.

War rages on

The war will keep on raging and the regulations and the fees and the greed and the abusive tactics may not go away, but you are wising up. You are learning what to do and what not to do.

Instead of being "an army of one," you are becoming a Consumer Financial Protection Bureau of One.

You are donning the armor and taking up the weapons. You are looking out for Number One, you, and you are getting some cool tactics to use. If having a credit card means you get a new computer when yours dies within 90 days of purchase, you better believe you use that benefit of purchase protection and get some money back.

Use everything in your power to make things better for you. That's the *Debt Cures* way.

CHAPTER 16

Student Loans

"There are approximately 37 million student loan borrowers with outstanding student loans today."
—Federal Reserve Board of New York

FinAid.org, which researches financial aid, estimates that student debt, compounded by rising enrollments, is growing by nearly $3,000 a second.

$3,000 every second. Tick. Tick. Tick.

The student loan world is taking on the tragic proportions and stories that has been the world of the housing market and foreclosures. It is out of control.

There's a lot of speculation that college debt is the next bubble after housing, the latest sector in which prices leap above real value.

Average student loan debt is near $30,000 and it keeps going up every year. The cost of college is a crime. Folks cannot find jobs so they go to school, hoping that at graduation time things will have shifted. They can't get work and they have to pay back the loans and there is no money to pay. People are living with their parents and they can't do it.

Default rate on student loans is also increasing all the time.

Student loan crisis

The Center for Responsible Lending reported that a new bill had been introduced into Congress. The Earnings Contingent Education Loans (ExCEL) Act of 2012 was modeled after similar student loan repayment plans that have enjoyed great success in the United Kingdom, Australia, and New Zealand.

Under this bill, student loan holders would pay a percentage of their income—automatically deducted from paychecks along with state and federal taxes—until their student loan is resolved. They would never pay greater than 15 percent of their income beyond an allowance for basic living expenses. If they get laid off, get sick, or face other hardships, the loan payments would be adjusted.

The representative who presented the bill states: "This approach protects borrowers from the financial ruin that comes with student loan default."

Too many folks have faced financial ruin because of student loan default.

Time will tell what becomes of this bill and any others. There are some versions of income-based repayment plans and some come with forgiveness of debt after a certain number of years, like 25. It seems gut-wrenching to think you have to pay on your school loans for twenty-five years and still not have them paid off.

What kind of country are we living in?

Crazy Rules

To muck it up even more, the current tax law says that forgiveness of debt is taxable income to you. So, on the one hand, the government will say you don't have to repay that remaining balance. Then on the other hand, the government says we will make you pay tax on what we just told you that you didn't have to pay.

You can't afford to repay the loans; the government understands that, so they forgive the debt after you have been paying all those years. The tax code says big deal, you gotta pay.

Again, I ask, what kind of country are we living in?

A pretty messed up one. One that has college tuition being totally unreasonable, for starters.

There are currently about two million people in this kind of repayment program, not sure of what will happen when the end of the repayment happens. The OMB runs some numbers showing that the average debt being repaid in such programs is $39,500. After all those years of repayment, the balance still due that could be forgiven would be over $41,000.

> ...the current tax law says that forgiveness of debt is taxable income...

Yes, that's more than the original loan balance. All those years of paying interest didn't do much to pay off the balance. All those years of paying and to still get stuck with taxes on over forty grand seems a bit out of whack.

Stay tuned. What will happen? Got a crystal ball?

Huge debt

The numbers are not getting any better. Last year, over ten million students took out federal student loans. Student loan debt is over $1 TRILLION.

The students are in crisis trying to repay, and also all the parents who took out loans to help their kids are in crisis trying to repay. There are even grandparents who are hurting because they helped out their grandkids.

The New York Times reported: "The number of borrowers of student loans age 60 and older was 2.2 million, a figure that has tripled since 2005. That makes them the fastest-growing age group for college debt. All told, those borrowers owed $43 billion, up from $8 billion seven years ago, according to the Federal Reserve Bank of New York."

Almost 10 percent of the borrowers over 60 were at least 90 days delinquent on their payments during the first quarter of 2012. And more and more of those with unpaid federal student debt are losing a portion of their Social Security benefits to the government.

The federal government does not track how many of these older borrowers were taking out loans for their own education rather than for that of their children. Financial analysts say that loans for children are the likely source of almost all the debt. Parent PLUS loans have more than doubled to $10.4 billion since 2000.

Colleges often encourage parents to get Parent PLUS loans, to make it possible for their children to attend that school. Many parents borrow more than they can afford to pay back— and discover, too late, that the flexibility of income-based repayment is available only to student borrowers.

How and when a parent can retire is being affected. Some folks have filed bankruptcy. Student loans do not get discharged in bankruptcy, but they spent everything they had to pay off the student obligations.

All because student loans are out of control.

Out of control

One TRILLION dollars. Another report stated: Student load debt is growing at a 20 percent-per-year pace. Since President Obama nationalized the industry (a tacked-on provision of the Obamacare bill), tuition has gone up 25 percent and the three-year default rate is at a record 13.4 percent.

Some say the answer is to return student loans to the private sector. There are no easy answers.

The interest rate on subsidized federal student Stafford loans taken out as of July 1, 2012, will remain at 3.4 percent for one more year. This was a last-minute Congressional decision. The interest rate was set by law to double to 6.8 percent this year.

Under a temporary provision that lasts until July 1, 2014, holders of subsidized Stafford loans will no longer enjoy an interest-free grace period after graduation. Historically, the federal subsidy extended for six months after a student completed school, meaning students would never pay for the half year of accruing interest.

For the next two years, students with subsidized student Stafford loans still won't have to start repayment until six months after they graduate, but interest will accrue during that time period.

Know the deal

Students really need to know what they are getting in to.

Graduate students are no longer eligible for government-subsidized Stafford loans. Grad students can still take out unsubsidized Stafford loans, for which interest accrues at a rate of 6.8 percent during school.

...850,000 loans in default.

Graduate students with federal loans will be eligible for the government loan repayment programs after graduation, including Income-Based Repayment and Public Service Loan Forgiveness, as well as unemployment deferment. Private lenders do not offer these kinds of benefits.

American Student Assistance keeps track of the stats. Nearly 20 million Americans attend college each year. Of the total one trillion bucks outstanding, roughly $864 billion is outstanding federal student loan debt while the remaining $150 billion is in private student loans.

About one-quarter of borrowers owe more than $28,000; 10% of borrowers owe more than $54,000; 3% owe more than $100,000.

Of the 37 million borrowers who have outstanding student loan balances, 14%, or about 5.4 million borrowers, have at least one past due student loan account. Approximately $85 billion is past due.

For every student loan borrower who defaults, at least two more borrowers become delinquent without default. Two out of five student loan borrowers—or 41%—are delinquent at some point in the first five years after entering repayment. As of 2012, there are now more than $8 billion in defaulted private loans, or 850,000 loans in default.

48% of 25-34 year-olds say they're unemployed or under-employed. 42% of those under 35 have more than $5,000 in personal debt that does not include a mortgage. 70% say it has become harder to make ends meet over the past four years.

I would say 100% of us would agree that for most, it has become harder to make ends meet over the last four years.

What is the government doing about all this?

"Concerned"

The U.S. Department of Education states: "We continue to be concerned about default rates and want to ensure that all borrowers have the tools to manage their debt," said U.S. Secretary of Education.

Thanks for your concern. It really seems to be helping. $1 trillion in debt and much of that in default.

From the fed's web site (ed.gov): "To help students access the tools and resources they need to avoid the negative consequences of defaulting on their student loans, the Department has redoubled its efforts to make borrowers aware of their student loan repayment options, including plans like Income-Based Repayment, which allows borrowers to cap their monthly student loan payments at 15 percent of their discretionary income.

The Department also recently released an interactive financial aid counseling tool that helps borrowers with their college financing decisions, including information on flexible loan repayment options. For more information on Income-Based Repayment and the online counseling tool, students can visit www.studentaid.gov."

Redoubled its efforts to make borrowers aware of a repayment plan. That repayment plan that may cause a big tax bill.

The CFPB is getting involved. The Consumer Financial Protection Bureau report called for increased regulation on private student loans, and included asking Congress to consider allowing borrowers to discharge those loans during bankruptcy.

Wouldn't that be interesting?

Bankruptcy and student loans

Some suggest that bankruptcy judges be allowed to wipe out ALL education debt. That was until 1976 when Congress began to tighten restrictions.

Federal Stafford loans are available to all undergraduate and graduate students, yet for some students, it isn't enough and they have to take private loans, too. Right now, any student loan cannot be discharged in bankruptcy.

There needs to be better education on the costs of education. Students are going into it not really knowing the score. Colleges want them to enroll so they give out forms with aid and loans and do not make it clear what has to be repaid and how much and for how long.

The Education Department is developing a form that colleges can use to give prospective students standardized information about how much they will owe upon graduation, what the school's loan-default and graduation rates are, and so on. Congress is fighting to make such a form mandatory, but so far it is still in the works, not a done deal.

Bloomberg BusinessWeek said it directly: "The most straightforward way to deal with the student debt problem is to bring down the unreasonably high cost of higher education, which forces students to go into debt in the first place."

Amen.

The economiccollapseblog.com gave some stats:

- ✔ Since 1978, the cost of college tuition in the United States has gone up by over 900%.

- ✔ Approximately two-thirds of all college students graduate with debt.

- ✔ According to the Economic Policy Institute, the unemployment rate for college graduates younger than 25 years old was 9.3 percent in 2010.

The old days of go to college and get a good job seem to be a thing of the past.

For those already in the trenches with student loan debt, you can go to the Department of Education site for free online calculators athttp://www2.ed.gov/offices/OSFAP/DirectLoan/calc.html. Visit studentloans.gov and use https://www.nslds.ed.gov/nslds_SA/ for the National Student Loan Data System.

This web site is where the government has put all of your student loan information in one place. You'll find a listing of all your student loan information including the name of your student debt servicers, your interest rate information and a clear picture of all your student loans in one place.

For student debt repayment assistance, go to the CFPB at http://www.consumerfinance.gov/paying-for-college/repay-student-debt/#Question-1. They give guidance as to your best next step in getting your payment in place.

For information on income based repayment, go to the Office of Financial Aid at http://studentaid.ed.gov/repay-loans/understand/plans/income-based. www.Studentloans.gov provides what the federal government provides. You can find out about direct loans at http://www.direct.ed.gov/.

CHAPTER 17

Foreclosures

*"Estimated $7 TRILLION total loss in home
equity resulting from the foreclosure crisis."*
—Center for Responsible Lending

We have been talking about foreclosures for years. For years! It
has gone beyond ridiculous. It is a crying shame.

Greed is not good. Greed causes havoc for many innocent
people.

Years ago, a foreclosure was a random and sad occurrence. Now
it is a common and sad occurrence.

I bet you know someone who has faced foreclosure. I bet you
know of many properties sitting empty in your town due to foreclosure. Many sit empty for years before they go on the market.

There is a glut of foreclosures and processing is slow. Especially
because the folks doing the processing are the idiots who created
the mess in the first place, and then in their greed and haste, made
it worse.

Things are not getting better.

Look at the table from statisticsbrain.com:

Year	Foreclosures	Foreclosure Filings	Home Repossessions
2013 (est.)	750,000	800,000	500,000
2012	2,100,000	2,304,941	671,000
2011	3,920,418	3,580,000	1,147,000
2010	3,843,548	3,500,000	1,125,000
2009	3,457,643	2,920,000	945,000
2008	3,019,482	2,350,000	679,000
2007	2,203,295	1,260,000	489,000
2006	1,215,304	545,000	268,532
2005	801,563	530,000	
2004	640,000		
2003	660,000		
2002	700,000		
2001	540,000		
2000	470,000		

For 2012, the actual numbers of foreclosures was still over two million. That many filings are still going on, too.

And, who says we are in recovery?

That's a bunch of bull. We are still hurting.

Recovery?

In California alone, about 500 people EVERY SINGLE DAY lose their home and this rate has not let up for the past FIVE YEARS!

California is on the top of the "leader board" when it comes to foreclosures. There is no light at the end of the tunnel. About one-third of homeowners are still underwater in their mortgages, too. Prices have not rebound. Signs of a return to "normal" are nowhere in sight, for California or the rest of the country.

States and counties now make it normal operating procedure to report and keep stats on the foreclosure inventory. You can go online and type in your city name, or any city name, and the word "foreclosure" to find out completed foreclosures, those pending, those filing, and there is the whole housing market of foreclosure properties.

It has become the new normal.

At year-end 2012, the Center for Responsible lending joined with Financial Services Roundtable and Housing Policy Council to ask Congress to extend the Mortgage Forgiveness Debt Relief Act.

> Signs of a return to "normal" are nowhere in sight...

Their letter to the boys in Washington says:

"Passed in 2007, the Mortgage Forgiveness Debt Relief Act prevents struggling and delinquent homeowners from having to pay taxes on any portion of their mortgage debts forgiven by financial institutions through short sales, principal forgiveness, or loan modifications.

Without the act, homeowners receiving such assistance would be required to pay income tax on the amount of debt forgiven, making it more difficult and expensive for these homeowners, who are already financially struggling, to accept short sales and many loan modification offers."

There are 97 institutions that make up the Financial Services Roundtable and the Center for Responsible Lending is a nonprofit whose primary focus is to fight predatory lending practices.

What is a predator?

Isn't it crazy that we have to have agencies, and institutions, and centers to fight predatory lending practices? The credit lending industry is a pack of predators. Predator is defined as: An organism that lives by preying on other organisms; or one that victimizes, plunders, or destroys, especially for one's own gain.

You do not have to be the victim anymore, and they sure do not get to destroy you. They try, have tried, and will continue to try, but you are wiser by the moment. No more plundering happening on your turf, on your watch.

The world is still in shambles. The greed that started a few years ago among the lenders handing out subprime mortgages created an avalanche of trouble. The economy has yet to fully rebound. Housing market still struggles. Foreclosures still happening. The predators still looking for prey.

Back in 2009, it made news that one of the big dog CEOs of one of the big mortgage companies agreed to pay fines of almost 2.5 million bucks to settle charges of fraud amid the mortgage meltdown.

The report stated: "The former head of American Home Mortgage Investment Corp. has agreed to pay nearly $2.5 million to settle federal civil charges of accounting fraud and concealing the company's deteriorating finances as the subprime mortgage crisis." Other charges included misleading investors and accounting fraud.

The major players in the national mortgage meltdown were these guys, the ones who thought they could get rich and to hell with everyone else. The country's top mortgage lenders led us down the wild path and we are still recovering.

Fallout continues

It's been more than five years now and the fallout continues. Their mistakes and yet we are the ones that keep paying.

The collapse in the mortgage world way back in 2007 launched the global economic crisis. These big dog bankers would not admit to wrongdoing, of course, but would agree to settle for millions. It seems to me that no one would pay out millions if they were not guilty. If you were innocent, would you agree to pay back millions?

This particular executive from American Home Mortgage was also barred for five years from serving as an officer or director of any public company. Those five years will soon be running out. Wonder where he will pop up again.

Do you want a guy like this, who hid losses and created "fictional profits" and deceived investors, and, in general, was an uncaring scumbag, running your company? Of course not. The credit world was filled with guys like that.

Fraud among the big dogs is common. That's what they are. The cases of mortgage fraud are ridiculous. They gave out loans back in 2006 without verifying the borrower's income. Take the money and run, and leave America holding the bag.

Thank you, greedy bastards.

Corporate greed

It used to be hard to believe that people could act in such a despicable way, but we see it over and over again now. The proof is before our very eyes. Corporate greed is at epidemic proportions. Out of control and reckless. The bankers and mortgage lenders have showed it over and over again.

Countless people lost their homes. Millions. Foreclosures have been at record highs for years now. The housing market has still not recovered. Folks who didn't lose their homes are underwater in their mortgages. People cannot sell because they wouldn't get enough money to pay off the mortgage. Folks are losing their jobs and not able to make the house payment and being foreclosed or walking away. Home values keep declining. The cycle does not seem to end. We have been talking the same story now since 2007.

> The cycle does not seem to end...same story now since 2007.

And, it all started with these lenders being greedy and corrupt. And, how does it go? Let's see, SEC charges of misleading investors and accounting fraud and cooking the books, and the guy does not go to jail.

Hmm, business school basics would seem to teach that before you give a loan, you find out the person's income and the ability to pay back the loan. It seems like common sense, but common sense can take a leave of absence when greed takes over.

The bigwigs wanted money, plain and simple. They did whatever they wanted and gave out loans to folks who, in reality, needed credit counseling, not a mortgage that was too big for them to afford. The execs had no interest in anything but lining their own pockets. Now our economy is in shambles. Still.

Hope?

Various home programs came forth from the government. Hope for Homeowners, created in July of 2008, created no hope.

This so-called housing rescue plan was to guarantee up to $300 billion worth of mortgages and to prevent more than 300,000 foreclosures.

This was, of course, after hundreds of thousands of foreclosures had already taken place. The plan was intended to be a stop-gap measure. To participate, banks had to take steep losses and their participation was voluntary. Gee, what a great plan.

How about a little bit of regulation that forces the banks to comply? How about a little bit of regulation in the beginning that would have noticed that the banks were handing out bogus loans?

No surprise, but the Hope for Homeowners plan was a bust. If you go online to http://www.hopeforhomeownersprogram.org/ you will see a notice that reads: This loan program was supposed to help over 400,000 households from pending foreclosure. It has not! Banks refuse to deliver the program to the public and have chosen to offer various loan modification programs instead. 300 Billion dollars is still sitting in the US Treasury...

From the get-go, it was a failure. The deal started October 1, 2008 and in early 2009, not a single loan had been worked out through this program. It should have been renamed Little Hope for Homeowners.

Create a government program and then not enforce it? What the heck?

This program phased out at the end of 2011. This site points you to other alternatives now. KnowYourOptions.com by Fannie Mae. MakingHomeAffordable.gov. HopeNow.com. You can call 888-995-HOPE to talk to someone at that hotline.

At Making Home Afforable.com, they announce that they are an official program of the Departments of Treasury and Housing & Urban Development (HUD). There are some programs out there online that are not government programs. There are many scamsters out there. Always be on the lookout. The help you need is usually free.

Improve the economy, please

The site proclaims: "The Making Home Affordable Program is a critical part of the Obama Administration's broad strategy to help homeowners avoid foreclosure, stabilize the country's housing market, and improve the nation's economy.

Eligible homeowners can lower their monthly mortgage payments and get into more stable loans at today's low rates. And for those homeowners for whom ownership is no longer affordable or desirable, the program can provide a way out which avoids foreclosure."

One program is called HARP—Home Affordable Refinance Program. Another is HAMP, which stands for Home Affordable Modification Program. Refinance differs from Modification. When you refinance, you are taking out a new loan to pay off the current one. A modification means you modify the current mortgage to make the terms better.

Loan modifications were not common at all before the crisis happened. The predators created a whole new wave in the industry.

Another program is called Home Affordable Unemployment Program—UP. Another is called Home Affordable Foreclosures Alternatives Program—HAFA.

You can get the nitty gritty on all these programs at http://www.makinghomeaffordable.gov/.

To beware of scammers, they give the following tips:

- ✔ "There should never be a fee for assistance with or information about the Making Home Affordable Program.

- ✔ Beware of any person or organization that asks you to pay an upfront fee in exchange for a counseling service or modification of a delinquent loan. Do not pay—walk away!

- ✔ Beware of anyone who says they can "save" your home if you sign or transfer over the deed to your house. Do not sign over the deed to your property to any organization or individual unless you are working directly with your mortgage company to forgive your debt.

- ✔ Never make your mortgage payments to anyone other than your mortgage company without their approval."

Scam victims

If you have been the victim of a scam, they advise:

- ✔ First, get the help you need to avoid foreclosure. Contact your servicer immediately.

- ✔ Contact a HUD-approved housing counselor through the Homeowner's HOPETM Hotline at 888-995-4673.

- ✔ Report the scam at
  - o https://www.ftccomplaintassistant.gov/
  - o http://www.loanscamalert.org/report-scams.aspx

- ✔ To learn more about foreclosure rescue or loan modification scams, go to http://www.makinghomeaffordable.gov/learn-more/Pages/beware.aspx

If you are having trouble with your house payment, you can call the hotline for guidance. They suggest you be prepared with as much information as possible so they can help you as much as possible. Have your paperwork ready. The site says to have:

- ✔ Monthly mortgage statement

- ✔ Information about other mortgages on your home, if applicable

- ✔ Two most recent pay stubs for all household members contributing toward mortgage payment

- ✔ Last two years of tax returns

- ✔ If self-employed, the most recent quarterly or year-to-date profit and loss statement

- ✔ Documentation of income you receive from other sources (alimony, child support, social security, etc.)

- ✔ Two most recent bank statements

- ✔ A utility bill showing homeowner name and property address

- ✔ Unemployment insurance letter, if applicable

- ✔ Account balances and minimum monthly payments due on all of your credit cards

- ✔ Information about your savings and other assets

- ✔ It may also be helpful to have: A letter describing any circumstances that caused your income to be reduced or expenses to be increased (job loss, divorce, illness, etc.) if applicable

If you are already working in the system to get your mortgage problems averted and things are still not going as well as you would like, or you have additional questions or need assistance following up with your mortgage servicer, call 888-995-HOPE (4673) and ask for "MHA° Help" to escalate your case.

The courts were, and still are, overrun with foreclosure proceedings. The banks were handling things very sloppily and that whole mess was yet another reason for the creeps to hang their heads in shame. They were processing people through with no care or regard and no good paperwork.

The tactic we shared in the earlier *Debt Cures* still stands. Do not let them steamroll you. If the bank or mortgage lender is taking you to court, make them show the documentation. Judges now are sick of the jerks pushing shoddy paperwork through.

Show me the papers

The magic words to remember in the case of foreclosure proceedings are Produce the Note.

No note. No deal.

If they cannot show proper documentation, they do not deserve to haul you into court. Plain and simple. Yet it was happening. Frequently.

This is how it works. The banks enter into mortgages with customers like you and then they sell off the mortgages in bundles to mortgage service companies or another bank or investment house.

That actual piece of paper called your mortgage can get lost in the shuffle somewhere. The holder of your mortgage account may not actually hold your note.

Even if they did not have the physical document, they were starting foreclosure proceedings.

If they didn't have the piece of paper documenting that you indeed owe, you bought yourself some time and a little time may be all you need.

The courts were buried with foreclosure cases. Most judges do not want to be bothered with the ones that are hassles. They have had it up to their eyeballs in foreclosure proceedings and want them to be clean.

> This has worked for many, many people.

If you show up in court knowing to demand that the lender produce the note, the stall tactic can give you several more months. While the mortgage holder is searching through the mountains of mortgages to find your note, you can be working your systems to find any way possible to raise the funds to pay on your mortgage and get caught up.

Does this tactic mean that you don't have to pay your mortgage? No. It means that the foreclosure proceedings of your case can be shelved for a few months. Time is on your side. This has worked for many, many people.

If the judge thinks the paperwork is incomplete or inaccurate, he or she can dismiss your foreclosure proceeding. According to a report by the Wall Street Journal, judges all across the country are taking their time and giving the documents a thorough look.

If there are mistakes, the judge does not have to accept the case. The whole system came to a near stand-still because so many cases were messed up. Fraudulent, abusive practices in the mortgage process got the whole crisis-ball rolling and fraudulent, abusive practices snowballed during the foreclosure craze.

They never learn. Some resources for you if you have trouble with your mortgage:

- ✔ http://www.federalreserve.gov/consumerinfo/foreclosure.htm

- ✔ http://www.usa.gov/Citizen/Topics/Family/Homeowners/Foreclosure.shtml

- ✔ http://portal.hud.gov/hudportal/HUD?src=/topics/avoiding_foreclosure

- ✔ http://www.consumer.ftc.gov/articles/0187-when-paying-mortgage-struggle

If you have an FHA mortgage:

- ✔ Call the National Service Center at (877) 622-8525 or

- ✔ Call the FHA Outreach Center at 1-800-CALL FHA (800-225-5342)

If you are facing issues with your house payment, and you have nowhere else to turn, go to your local HUD office. They can steer you to a counselor, for free, who can help you sort it all out. To find the office nearest you, go to www.hud.gov or call 800-569-4287.

CHAPTER 18

The Upside of Foreclosures

"House flipping died with the housing boom,
right? Wrong."
—*Chicago Magazine*

Illinois was in the top five states that have been hardest hit by the foreclosure garbage, and here *Chicago Magazine* writes about how well the flipping market is doing. That article was written at year-end 2012. As of the writing of this book, the housing market is still weak. Flipping still works.

During the housing boom, many people used to buy homes (foreclosed or not), fix them, and sell them quickly for a nice little profit. Flipping houses was a cottage industry, pardon the pun.

Then with so many foreclosures coming on the market, and the prices fizzling for resale, and the market in general being a breeding ground for fear, things sort of went haywire for a bit. Yet it is still game to make money off of foreclosures, even in this economy, even in this market. Savvy folks are taking part.

The average profit on a flip house was nearly $30,000. The average home is flipped in just over 100 days. Nearly two-thirds of the buyers of the flip houses are first-time home buyers, thrilled to have a house.

At the close of last year, the best places for flipping were Seattle; San Jose; Richmond, VA; Philadelphia; Raleigh, NC; Omaha; Washington, DC; Oxnard, CA; Lake Havasu City; and New York, NY.

One couple bought their first foreclosed property in Texas in 2008. They got it for a song, $50,000. They spent another $60,000 fixing it up. They sold it, yes they did, for $175,000. Do the math. That is a $65,000 deal.

Flip for funds

Many people are making big money.

A year-end 2012 article in *Chicago Magazine* gave this advice: "When evaluating a potential deal, add the purchase price to the amount it will realistically take to turn the place into a desirable property. (Establish relationships with reliable contractors who can estimate the cost of turning a place around and have the experience to deliver the goods while sticking to a budget.) Only if the total comes in at least 20 percent below the present-day market price of similarly sized homes in the neighborhood is it worth going forward (though fix-up time and the state of the neighborhood could boost that percentage upward)." The same holds true today!

Always, before any transaction, you do the numbers. Does it make sense? Use your common sense and the wisdom of folks who know, like contractors, before you jump in and buy a flip house.

Another person bought a property for $130,000 that needed a lot of work. They did their homework before buying. They knew what it would take to get it in good shape. They knew what that area and market would bear for resale. This guy leapt and it paid off. He dumped another $200,000 into the house and was able to sell it for $417,000.

Nice money.

The flipping experts say buying a home in poor condition is often the way to go. You can get a great deal and the fix-up costs pay for themselves.

The trick is to be patient. Look at dozens and dozens of houses before you leap. Know that a good flip is a good deal and finding the right house takes time. Don't get hooked on a house either. Some properties that are deemed to be good flip projects get a lot of bidders. Do not get in a bidding war. Your aim is to get a low price. Be ready to walk away and let that house go to some other guy. There are plenty out there for you.

The experts also suggest that the best flip deals are houses, not condos. There is a glut of condos for sale now and good deals can be had. Look into those for rental potential. Not all condo buildings allow that though. Be smart. Be savvy. Be patient.

Don't freak out if you take a loss on a house too. If you are doing many flips, the odds are that something will happen and you will not get the price you want on a house in the end. Don't despair. Know that your profits from the others will absorb this loss.

Learn lessons from whatever happened and move on. An occasional loss is not a reason to stop flipping.

Flip finds

To start your search, you can use the realty web sites like www.realtor.com or www.zillow.com to find inexpensive properties. Find something in your price range and get a good estimate of what fixing it up will cost.

Know what you will do and what you will hire out. Expect things to go a little over budget from what you are quoted, so keep that in your game plan.

Profits can be great. There are low cost homes everywhere and not necessarily in low cost neighborhoods. People of all income brackets have faced foreclosure. Homes with $300,000 plus mortgages had homeowners who could not make the payments, and ended up losing their homes.

> Be realistic about renovation costs and the hidden expense…

The foreclosure crisis affected all income brackets, all education levels, all races, all areas, all states. Which means opportunities are everywhere.

You can get into a high-end area and buy some properties at prices that were unheard of just a couple years back.

Florida was second to California in the hardest-hit stats. The Orlando paper reported: "It may seem counterintuitive to invest in real estate when the housing market is in its darkest hour. But in fact, it may prove to be the most optimal time for such a venture. Home flippers can still find plenty of opportunities."

Angie Hicks, of the famous internet site angieslist.com, knows about this too. She said: "The key…is doing your research and knowing what you're getting into. Know the area you're buying in, the market, how the price compares to the neighborhood."

Know what you like and let that be a guide. One expert finds house flip bargains mostly in neighborhoods where she would like to live.

Areas undergoing urban renewal also are good investment opportunities.

One experienced flipper says that in the recent past many flippers found themselves in trouble because they had not correctly calculated the amount of money it takes to finish a flip and market it. Know how much money you'll need right up front, and not just the purchase price. Be realistic about renovation costs and the hidden expense of carrying costs—that is what gets so many into trouble.

Most houses take longer now than 60 days to flip. Know that going into the deal. Understand that you will be making some house payments in the interim. That has to be factored into your projected profit.

Flip finances

For those serious about flipping and who want to get a bank loan, plan on having 25% down. The strategy folks are using now is to aggressively low ball on prices. Offer even lower than what you would have on a property just a year or so ago. The lower you can get a property, the better your profit.

Some flippers are getting their real estate agent license too so they do not have to pay a realtor commission when they sell the flips. Being able to pocket the commission leads to a greater profit, too, on each house sold.

Remember the golden rule of any home purchase, especially a foreclosure: Always inspect the property yourself. Always research the title. You don't want any surprises. And, do not ever overpay.

If you are entering the world of foreclosures, be ready to learn the terms that are used. Ever heard of junior liens or senior liens? Liens are basically the mortgages on the property. The senior lien is the first mortgage and the one with the most clout. That is the one you want. A mistake people make is that they buy a junior lien and not a senior lien.

The guy holding the senior lien is the guy with the trump cards. If you do not do a title search and buy a junior lien, you could be out the entire amount that you paid.

And if you are buying a foreclosure, or any property that you plan to turn around and sell for a profit, you need to make sure to pay the taxes and the insurance on the property during the time you own it.

There are several kinds of properties that you can find at a good price. You can ask your local bank for a list. Some government agencies, as well as the banks, have foreclosed properties. Try HUD or VA defaulted loan properties, Fannie Mae and Freddie Mac defaulted loan properties, default on taxes properties, and law enforcement seized properties. Talk to your local realtors and look at the web sites for your area.

Ask attorneys, real estate agents, and banks or mortgage companies. Look at foreclosure web sites, public record of divorce decrees, and foreclosure and bankruptcy notices in local papers, and simply ask around. Buy a house that is already vacant. You don't want to deal with folks still living there, not knowing when they will leave and what they will do the property.

Flip friends

Don't be intimidated if this is new to you. You need knowledge-able people to help you with foreclosures and real estate transac-tions. Ask your friends and family. Find a trusted home inspector, real estate agent, a real estate attorney, an accountant, and a title company expert. If you are not a handyman, get someone who is or hire a contractor. They can give you an idea of how much repairs will cost before you make the commitment to buy the rental property or foreclosed home.

You can rely on the expertise of others and it can make the whole process much smoother, and in the end, more profitable. Your goal is to make 20% return on investment. Many people make much more.

> ... rely on the expertise of others and it can make the whole process smoother...more profitable.

When it comes time to sell, get an agent you like and trust. Make sure the house has curb appeal. Clean up the yard and clean the whole house. Have a clean, welcoming front door. Tell everyone you know about this little gem of a house that you fixed up to sell and it is priced to sell, too. Set a good price and never underestimate word of mouth selling.

Also, be prepared to be a landlord. Many people are buying flip houses and if they don't sell, you rent it instead. Houses command good rent and the demand is huge. Many people do not have down payments to buy a house or their credit is shaky, yet they want to live in a nice house. You can work a deal and have rental income every month paying all the expenses of owning the property plus a profit for you.

Either way, flip houses are a money maker for you.

Flip success

One *Debt Cures* reader named Ramanda now makes $35,000 from renting and flipping, and "not lifting a finger."

It can be easy money. Rental property has been the start of many a millionaire.

Maybe you think you do not have the funds to start playing the flip game. If you find yourself with not much on the side to get started, consider all your options to round up some cash. Revisit the fast money ideas. Consider OPM, other people's money.

Because of OPM, you can buy property no matter what your financial situation is, no matter what your credit score is, and no matter how much cash you have in the bank. You can start working your way into wealth with no cash outlay of your own. Using other people's money is brilliant and you can do it, too.

Take for example, you found a rental property that you wanted to invest in. The seller agreed to carry the financing. Your poor credit was not an issue in getting a loan because the seller was playing the part of the bank. Your loan was with him. He knew that you could afford the monthly payment and you reached an agreement.

You and the seller entered into a contract for the property. The seller then partnered back with you, keeping 50% ownership for himself. So even with lousy credit, you became 50% owner of an investment rental property.

Part of the deal was to become the manager of the properties as well. Great. Say after two years of managing the properties, you then sold back two units to the seller, and kept one in your ownership. You made $80,000 on the deal! $80,000 in two years is a good return on investment, wouldn't you say? That is a nice sum for someone who had a very bleak credit score. That is a nice sum for anyone.

You may be asking yourself, why would the seller finance the deal? Why not? Why would the seller do anything? There are hundreds of unique reasons why people do what they do. In this case, you agreed to be property manager.

Ask

You never know until you ask. The magic words of "would you be willing to" can be followed up with "finance this deal?" or "carry the contract?"

You can think up all kinds of things that a seller had not thought of at first. Do not be afraid to ask if there is anything the seller is willing to do to make the deal happen and be a good transaction for both of you.

In this case, the seller financed the deal and retained 50% ownership. It was a good deal for him. He had you take over half of the financial burden, which lightened his load financially, and you managed the rental properties, which freed him up to do other things with his time.

You never know when someone needs some cash and will carry the contract themselves. Maybe they don't even need the cash, but can see the benefit to both of you. Who knows what can happen. If you think that OPM is not going to happen for you, think again.

There are opportunities all around you, once you start looking for them. Other People's Money—it comes in unexpected places and in unexpected ways. Once you grasp the idea, and start asking, you'll be pleasantly surprised at the deals you can make—even if you have no money or no credit.

The golden rule of *Debt Cures* is always: ASK.

Build your wealth

Even while you are still in the process of ridding yourself of debt, you can move forward. These kinds of ventures are great avenues to building wealth. Like I have said a million times, for a million reasons, you never know until you ask.

Absolutely, you can take advantage of the current situation and make a fortune off of foreclosures. Don't feel guilty about it. You did not create this mess. The good old boys in Washington and the fat cat bankers can take the credit for this situation.

In 2006, when the whole housing crisis was beginning, over 50% of mortgages were with mortgage lending companies like mortgage brokers and finance companies. They were not subject to bank regulations.

We'll see what the CFPB implements as time goes by. They want to protect the consumer from the predators in the lending industry. Sharks. And, you can swim with them.

CHAPTER 19

Home = Money

"Decisions about how we spend our money determines how we live."
—Home & Money, Purdue University

Home sweet home.

Or so it should be.

With a traditional thirty-year mortgage, a homeowner ends up paying about double the purchase price of the home after those thirty years of interest have been paid.

That's not so sweet.

With a very simple method, you can pay less interest, and thus pay less on the very same mortgage. Same house, paid off quicker, paid off with less money out of your pocket. Sound appealing?

Mortgages are usually set up as a monthly payment. Let's say your mortgage is $1,000 per month. Due on the first of the month, you pay the full $1,000 and wait until next month to roll around, and you pay again. A simple secret: You can knock off tremendous interest expense by paying early.

The way interest calculations are made, prepaying has a huge impact. One easy way to pay early is to pay weekly.

The amount of your payment does not change; the same amount of money leaves your checkbook.

Seriously simple

You simply pay installments each week, so that by the first of the month, you have paid the entire amount due in full. In our example of $1,000, you would pay $250 each week. Your monthly expense is not changed at all, your budget is the same. All you do is change the timing of your payments.

It can save you thousands of dollars over the life of the mortgage. This method of prepayments also cuts the life of your 30-year mortgage, too, just by paying each week.

For those who get paid every week, this can be an easy switch to make. If you get paid every two weeks, you can do this prepayment method as well. Biweekly payments of $500 can be made.

All you do is change the timing of your payments.

Once Gloria Marie read about this method in *Debt Cures* she decided to make bimonthly payments on her mortgage. She will save $47,247 in interest payments. With a mortgage of $343,000 she would have paid $273,517.44 in interest. By using this method Gloria Marie has whittled that number down to $226,270 and says, "I am going to be able to save over $40,000 on my mortgage and pay off my house 6-10 years earlier…that's amazing. I'm in a house that I love, a family house, a house that I'm going to stay in. And, the idea that I will completely own it from the banks in a shorter amount of time is a dream come true."

The way the interest calculations are run, the prepayment amounts knock off some principal and the interest is thus compounding on a smaller balance. Less interest over the years and less years to pay. This also means more equity built up faster.

There are other simple ways to get your home paid off quicker. Even if you make just one extra mortgage payment each year, you can take as much as three years off the life of your loan. Some people make lump sum "bonus" payments against principal whenever they come into a little money, any time of year, in any amount, as often as they like.

Paying down the debt decreases the amount of interest that needs to be rung up. Even as little as $15 every two weeks applied to your mortgage can cut one and a half years off.

Some people simply pay more each month when the mortgage is due. If your house payment is $1,000 and you pay even a hundred dollars more each month, you make a big dent in the overall balance. Little things mean a lot and anything more on the mortgage has a compound effect. In your advantage.

Any change in your spending habits can be applied against the mortgage. Make sure that your mortgage allows the prepayment option. Most do, but be wise and double check before you follow this line of attack.

Numbers speak

Let's look at a quick example. Ginger has tackled the task of improving her credit report and now has a credit score of 720. She qualifies for an interest rate of 5.5%.

Mary Ann has been lying around watching reruns on television and waiting for a magic fairy to come hand over a winning lottery ticket. Her FICO score was 550, and the mortgage company gave her an interest rate of 9.3%.

They both took out $200,000 mortgages.

Ginger will have a monthly mortgage payment of $1,100. Mary Ann will have a monthly payment of around $1,650. She pays over $500 more each and every month. After a year that means she shelled out $6,600 more than Ginger.

If they both pay for thirty years, Mary Ann will pay $186,000 more in interest. That is nearly what the original mortgage amount was.

Let's say Mary Ann wised up and decided to pay off the mortgage early. That monthly amount due of $1,650 was paid in weekly installments of about $415, making sure that the full amount was paid by the first of every month.

This one small tactic saved her boatloads of money and cut the length of the mortgage, too.

Lose the PMI

Another way to save money on the house payment is to stop paying PMI. PMI (Private Mortgage Insurance) is a fee that the lenders collect until you, the homebuyer, have 20% equity in your home. It's a gimmick, a rip-off, a way for them to siphon more money out of you. PMI is money out the window. You don't want to pay it any longer than you have to.

If you are buying a home, find a way to make a 20% down payment so you do not have to pay PMI. If you do not have 20%

down, make sure that when you reach 20%, you contact the lender to remove this fee as they may or may not automatically do so. It is up to you to pay attention.

Refinancing can be a great way to reduce your payment and your overall interest expense. Usually, there is a fee to refinance your mortgage. Whatever the closing costs are can be divided by your monthly savings (your old payment amount compared to the new monthly payment after the re-fi) to determine how long it will take you to recover the fees associated with refinancing.

If you are going to be in your house a few years, it can be cost beneficial to do the refinance. Run the numbers yourself before you refinance, but in many cases, it's a good strategy for an immediate payment reduction and overall long-term savings.

Don't wait

If you are having trouble with your payment, talk to your lender right away. When the whole mortgage meltdown crisis started, banks were in foreclosure mode and didn't work with their home-owners. As the crazy crisis continued and the mortgage lenders were taking on too many homes in foreclosure and getting stuck with them, the idea of mortgage renegotiation became more appealing.

The banks have learned that taking back your house means they have to pay the taxes and the insurance, and wait for it to sell. Months and months of this made them open their eyes. Keeping you in the house, with a lesser payment, means income to them and you do not have to lose your house. Don't be afraid to ask for a renegotiation of your mortgage terms. It never hurts to ask. See what they can do for you.

People in all parts of the country, of all races, of all income levels, and of all education levels are now seeking mortgage renegotiation.

ONE MILLION mortgages have been renegotiated since this whole debacle began. I consider mortgage renegotiation another set of magic words.

People are getting house payments that are 40% lower than what they paid before. Some are getting 60% lower. By getting a payment that you can afford, you will keep your credit report in good standing.

The renegotiation itself does not get reported. All it means for you is that you have a payment that you are able to make so no late payments appear on the credit record. You are able to keep your house and keep your credit score intact.

With a renegotiation it is your same mortgage, so there are no fees involved like with a refinance. What the mortgage lender does is modify your current terms. Maybe you get a lower interest rate for a set amount of time. Maybe you get a lower payment and the length of the loan gets extended. Usually it is temporary, but some modifications remain for the life of the loan.

It is still the American dream to have a home, and to stay in our homes. There are ways to make this happen.

CHAPTER 20

Bankruptcy

*"Bankruptcies slipped again in the third quarter
of 2012, though experts do not expect the trend to
last much longer."*

—Creditcards.com

So, the "trend" of fewer bankruptcies is not expected to last.
That's a sad commentary on the state of our economy.

The Bankruptcy Abuse Prevention and Consumer Protection
Act of 2005 was created to reduce the number of bankruptcies. That
act meant higher filing fees, a test for eligibility, required counseling
programs and an eight-year moratorium before a person can file
for bankruptcy again.

Because people were freaked out about the tighter rules, TWO
MILLION people filed for bankruptcy in 2005 before the new
changes kicked in.

Then the economy crashed and burned. Folks filed for bankruptcy even with the more stringent rules. In 2007, there were
about 850,000 filings. The numbers have climbed ever since. So
much for that "consumer protection act."

The government in all its wisdom thought that folks were abusing the right to file bankruptcy, so they made the laws tougher. Why didn't they make the rules tougher on the folks running this country?

If you want to track the numbers of filings for each month, you can go online to web sites like https://www.nbkrc.com/Default.aspx for the National Bankruptcy Research Center (NBKRC) and American Bankruptcy Institute (ABI) at http://www.abiworld.org/.

Recent stats from http://news.uscourts.gov/show:

Business and Non-Business Filings
Years Ended March 31, 2009-2013

Year	Business	Non-Business	Total
2013	**37,552**	**1,132,772**	**1,170,324**
2012	**46,393**	**1,320,613**	**1,367,006**
2011	54,212	1,516,971	1,571,183
2010	61,148	1,470,849	1,531,997
2009	49,077	1,153,318	1,202,395

Source: http://news.uscourts.gov/bankruptcy-filings-down-fiscal-year-2012

When anywhere from one million to 1.5 million people are filing bankruptcy every year in this country, something is out of whack.

Recession over? Recovery? Anybody seen it?

Bankruptcy is tough. Most people have mixed emotions when it comes to bankruptcy. Most of the time, I say you can avoid it. But I also realize how common it is and that some of you may be thinking about it.

Bankruptcy protection

An old article in the USA Today from March 2009 still says it best: "Cash-strapped families are seeking bankruptcy protection at nearly the same rate and in the same manner as they did before the much-debated 2005 bankruptcy law reform, a trend critics say proves the reform was a failure. Congress wrangled for eight years before passing a reform act aimed at curbing abuse and ending an alarming rise in bankruptcy filings. With the economy in tatters and personal fortunes often in even worse shape these days, the bankruptcy law is beginning to undergo scrutiny again." (Source: http://usatoday30.usatoday.com/money/economy/2009-03-22-reform-filings-bankruptcy_N.htm)

The economy is still in tatters.

Bankruptcy law may still be under scrutiny, but not much is happening on that front. The wheels in Washington turn very slow.

> Bankruptcy filings have been on the rise again.

If you are facing bankruptcy or have filed, don't despair. Obviously, you are not alone. Millions stand with you.

Bankruptcy is not the end. I know many a millionaire with a bankruptcy filing in their past. It is more common than you think.

Because of the 2005 reform in the bankruptcy laws, what was supposed to "help" has really hindered. It costs more, takes longer and is more difficult to file now. And of course, the reform is better for the banks than the person filing for bankruptcy.

No surprise there.

People are struggling and cannot even afford to file for bankruptcy. What does that say about our policies?

In 2005, there was a record two million bankruptcy filings. What a sad commentary at the state of our union. Since the economy tanked, bankruptcy filings have been on the rise again. You saw the numbers. What does that say about our economy?

It stinks.

No shame

There is no shame in filing for bankruptcy. *USA Today* also reported: "One of the primary purposes of the bankruptcy law is to provide a way to grant debt relief to the honest-but-overextended debtor, who through no fault of his own is burdened by more debt than he can pay," says Sam Gerdano, executive director of the American Bankruptcy Institute, an independent research and education organization." (Source: http://usatoday30.usatoday.com/money/economy/2009-03-22-reform-filings-bankruptcy_N.htm)

There's no shame, but the 2005 law certainly makes it more of a pain to file for bankruptcy, especially for higher income folks. Those people have to pass a "means" test. They have to provide pages and pages of paperwork, from tax returns and pay stubs to other sources of income, plus a detailed listing of all expenses.

The government wants people to not file Chapter 7, which excuses most of the debt, including credit card balances, and instead file Chapter 13, which makes you pay all your debts still, just over an extended period of time.

The credit card companies cry because bankruptcy filings put a dent in their budget. They say bankruptcy issues made them lose billions of dollars. Poor babies. So what do they do? They up their fees to cover their losses.

The bankruptcy reform has actually helped the credit card industry. Now you tell me, who is in bed with whom? The credit card lobbyists have their pals in Washington make it harder for people to file bankruptcy. Not only do these people have to keep paying on their credit card bills and not get a clean slate, the credit card companies can keep racking them with fees and fees and fees.

Credit card profits

This is what the experts at Card Trak, a credit card research firm, have to say: "Since the reform passed, the credit card industry's profits have grown. It earned $19.9 billion from penalty fees in 2008, up from $14.8 billion in 2005, according to R.K. Hammer, a consulting firm. The industry's pretax profit climbed to about $39 billion in 2008 from $30.6 billion in 2005." (Source: http://usa-today30.usatoday.com/money/economy/2009-03-22-reform-fil-ings-bankruptcy_N.htm)

Those numbers may be a little old, but it does not matter. It shows that the credit card folks make BILLIONS in penalty fees and the efforts to "reform" only serve to keep putting coins in their coffers.

The credit card giants are making a profit off the cash-strapped hard working citizen. Same old song and dance.

The experts concur: "There has been no rollback on credit card fees," says Robert McKinley, founder of CardTrak.com. "Punitive rates are just as aggressive as they were before, even though the prime rate has dropped dramatically. In 2005, the punitive rate was 30.99% as the prime rate was up to 7.00%. Last year, the punitive credit card rate was 30.88%, but the prime rate was only 4.00%,... an unprecedented rate spread." (Source: http://usatoday30.

usatoday.com/money/economy/2009-03-22-reform-filings-bank-ruptcy_N.htm)

That same article quotes a Harvard Law School Fellow: "The data is unambiguous: 2005 Bankruptcy Reform benefited credit card companies and hurt their customers."

Some things never change

Same old, same old. It's a broken record. Things may seem to change, yet some things stay the same. The credit card companies get the benefit. The customers get the bill.

A bankruptcy judge of twenty-five years said, "The 2005 bill was the culmination of eight years and some $50 million of effort by the finance industry to screw honest debtors. The reference in the title to the legislation as a "Consumer Protection Act" was a fraud and a cruel joke. There are no consumer protections of significance in the Act. There are, however, numerous hurdles and costly measures that serve no purpose other than to shut out distressed individual debtors." Cruel jokes leave no one laughing.

Bankruptcy hits everyone.

An AARP study found that the increase in filings by folks age 55 and older was up an astonishing 78% over the last ten years. Harvard Law professor Elizabeth Warren was one of the researchers in the study. She states that in 1991, this age group accounted for about 8% of all bankruptcies. Now 25% of bankruptcy filings are those in their "golden years."

Sad.

Much too common

Bankruptcy is all too common. If you find that bankruptcy is your last option, here is what you need to know.

Get a lawyer. Find someone you trust. Ask around. This situation is more common than you may realize. Your friends, family, and neighbors can probably suggest a good bankruptcy attorney.

The ones who seem shady probably are; trust your gut. You want someone who is looking out for you, not out to make a buck off of you. There are tons that advertise on television and on the internet. They may or not be any good. Get a recommendation first, before you start to deal with him or her and especially before you give any money.

> ... you need to talk to a lawyer. You need to get your life back.

Bankruptcy should not be a rash decision. Think about it. Talk about it. Research your options. If you cannot make the house payment and the car payment, that's one factor. If you are not able to pay your bills and pay down on your debt, that's one factor. If you live in fear of answering the phone or opening your mail because you are hounded by collectors, that's one factor.

You need to weigh all the factors.

If you had a serious illness, or lost your job, or had a divorce, or a death, or some other "big" event that created a huge financial mess, you may need to consider bankruptcy. Some people think it is the only option; it is not, but it is an out sometimes.

Some people can't function when they are burdened with debt. If you are one of those people, you need to talk to a lawyer. You need to get your life back.

There are two kinds of individual bankruptcy, Chapter 7 and Chapter 13.

Chapter 7 is a basic liquidation of your assets. What you have is not enough cash value and cannot pay off what you owe, your liabilities. Chapter 13 bankruptcy is called a personal reorganization. With this plan, you pay back your debts over three to five years with a court-approved arrangement.

The type of bankruptcy that you file depends upon your income and your assets and if you want to keep your house. The bankruptcy reform of 2005 wants more people to file Chapter 13 (obviously) instead of letting you wipe the slate clean.

It used to be that if you filed bankruptcy, you had to wait seven years until you could file again. The reform changed the time span to eight years. But with all this kind of legal stuff, check with your attorney.

Filing for bankruptcy does show up as a negative item on the credit report. But if you feel bankruptcy is the way to go, you can overcome the credit score hit over time.

Still will owe

You also have to remember that filing bankruptcy does not give you a clean slate of all debt owed. If you have student loans or owe money to the IRS, you still have to pay those debts. Some things just don't go away.

Take out a piece of paper and list all your assets. List everything that you owe money on. How does it look?

You can have an accountant draw up an income statement and balance sheet for you or you can do a rough draft yourself.

Another word for bankrupt is insolvent. That doesn't sound quite so intimidating, does it? You decide if being insolvent means talking to a bankruptcy lawyer or if it means pursuing other options.

Where there is a will to succeed, there is a debt cure to fit the bill. If bankruptcy is what fits your bill, don't stress about it. There have been many millionaires with a bankruptcy in their past. It's not a life sentence. It's one growing pain.

According to uscourts.gov, "Bankruptcy laws help people who can no longer pay their creditors get a fresh start—by liquidating assets to pay their debts or by creating a repayment plan."

Think of it as a fresh start.

Many successful, wealthy and wise people overcame bankruptcy. You can, too. You can join the likes of Walt Disney, Henry Ford, Donald Trump, A.J. Heinz, George Foreman, Milton Hershey, Larry King, Francis Ford Coppola, Ulysses S. Grant, P.T. Barnum, William McKinley, and Abraham Lincoln.

Yes, Honest Abe overcame bankruptcy. You can, too.

CHAPTER 21

Tax Credits

*"A tax credit is a sum deducted from the total
amount a taxpayer owes."*
—Wikipedia

That's right. A tax credit reduces your tax. You pay less to the government. That's a beautiful thing.

More money for you. Less money for Uncle Sam.

I am no fan of the Internal Revenue Service, no secret there. So whenever there is money available to you from the IRS and Uncle Sam, it is my thrill and delight to share that information with you.

Tax credits are, essentially, a gift from the government. Money is money, and money from the feds is somehow even better.

Tax credits are not new, but many people overlook them. You need to be aware of them and also stay on top of them. They come, they go, they expire, they get extended, they die away. Tax credits are always changing.

Cuts, hikes, slashes, spending…it all spells more money from the taxpaying public. The tax code is always changing, this time a lot of items were on the chopping block. And, things always will be. No matter when you pick up this book, always check with your tax advisor for the most current info. Make sure you get the best with what is in effect at the time.

The Tax Policy Center has online calculators for you to estimate your tax liability with several possible scenarios. Go to http:// calculator.taxpolicycenter.org/.

There are a lot of changes in the works, affecting a lot of tax credits. One of the biggest effects would be the change in the child tax credit. A cut from $1,000 per child to $500 per child is a big hit for many American families.

Higher tax bills

Many Americans will face higher tax bills. Estimates by tax policy groups and government accountants put the total tax cost at more than $500 billion in 2013.

That averages out to almost $3,500 per household, according to calculations by the Tax Policy Center. Middle-class taxpayers are likely to see an average increase of almost $2,000.

If any taxpayers have investments in a taxable brokerage account, their tax bills next year will be higher, too.

A lot was at stake for a lot of people in a lot of areas.

The middle class, as always, gets hit hard, too. Lower income folks are not saved from the fate either. Payroll taxes. Income taxes. It's all taxes.

On New Year's Day 2013, the "American Taxpayer Relief Act of 2012" (the Act) was enacted to avoid the impact of automatic "fiscal cliff" tax increases. In addition to higher tax rates for higher-income folks, under the Act, the new taxes under the Patient Protection and Affordable Care Act (Obamacare) went into effect in 2013: a new 3.8 percent tax applies to net investment income of taxpayers with modified adjusted gross incomes over $250,000 (married filing jointly), and a new additional Medicare tax of 0.9 percent is imposed on taxpayers with wages in excess of $250,000 (married filing jointly).

Take a look at your tax returns over the past several years. Were you able to claim a child tax credit? What about the Earned Income Tax Credit (EITC)? Were you married filing jointly and enjoying the fact that you were not penalized on your taxes because of it? Do you look at your W-2s and your paystubs? How has your take home pay changed over these last few years?

No matter your situation, be aware of every tax credit that you can get. The details may change, so check with your tax advisor, but claim every penny of credit you can. Get every break that you can.

Take those credits

Now more than ever, it is wise to really go over your records and make sure you have every deduction you can take and use every tactic to reduce your overall tax burden. Have a trusted accountant or tax professional discuss all the ways you can make the most of the current tax law, whatever that may turn out to be.

The tax laws are always changing.

There were credits that came about due to the American Recovery and Reinvestment Act, part of the first Obama administration. Visit www.Recovery.gov to learn more. This act, from the folks who wrote it, was "an unprecedented effort to jumpstart our economy, create or save millions of jobs, and put a down payment on addressing long-neglected challenges so our country can thrive in the 21st century."

> ...make sure you have every deduction...

They called it an extraordinary response to a crisis unlike any since the Great Depression. Recovery.gov stated: "With much at stake, the Act provides for unprecedented levels of transparency and accountability so that you will be able to know how, when, and where your tax dollars are being spent. Spearheaded by a new Recovery Board, this Act contains built-in measures to root out waste, inefficiency, and unnecessary spending. This web site, Recovery.gov, will be the main vehicle to provide each and every citizen with the ability to monitor the progress of the recovery."

Quite lofty.

Here we are, four years later, and the economy is still in need of a jumpstart. Folks are still in need of jobs. Those long-neglected challenges of our country are still hanging in the wind, and we are far from thriving in this new century.

The paragraph talking about transparency and accountability and knowing where tax dollars are being spent is lovely. It's BS, but it's lovely BS.

Have we rooted out waste, inefficiency, and unnecessary spending?

Has anything changed?

Are we in "recovery?"

I think not.

Typical government SNAFU. Situation Normal. All F'ed Up.

Take advantage

That said, even with things as they are, still be aware and take advantage of any tax credits that you can. Money you don't have to pay Uncle Sam is sweeter all the time.

Tax credits may change, but they still exist. Let's cover some of the most common ones here.

The child tax credit is simply a credit you get for having a qualifying child under the age of 17 at the end of the year who is your son, daughter, stepson, stepdaughter, legally adopted child, or a child placed with you for legal adoption, brother, sister, stepbrother, stepsister, foster child, or a descendant of any such person and lives with you in your principal residence for more than one-half of the tax year.

The IRS is wordy and complicates things, but in general, if you have a kid under age 17 who qualifies as your dependent and who lives with you more than half the time, you may get the credit.

To get all the details, refer to Publication 672. If you have questions, as always, call the IRS or look up www.irs.gov.

Currently, you get a credit of $1,000 per child. The change that was possibly coming with the fiscal cliff would have been just $500 per child.

With the passing of the deal, the amount of this credit was approved to remain at $1,000 for five years.

The credit is limited to income restrictions. The amount of credit phases out due to the more money you make. Ask your tax advisor or look up at irs.gov what the current limits are when you are doing your taxes.

Let's use an example where your credit is $1,000. If your tax due is $1,000, and you have a credit of $1,000, you apply the credit and dollar for dollar wipe out the tax. You owe nothing.

If your tax bill was $1,400, you would only owe $400. Make sense?

This credit is not refundable. That means if you owe $500 in tax and your credit is $1,000, you eliminate all tax, but you do not get the extra $500 refunded to you.

There are some credits that are refundable. Even if you owe no tax, you still get the full credit money.

To claim the child tax credit, you simply check a box on the front of the return where you enter the names and social security numbers of your children. There's a worksheet in the instruction booklet for the Form 1040 to compute the credit.

Even if you put money into an employer Flexible Spending Account (FSA), you might still be able to take the credit, too, depending on your circumstances. If you have two or more children and your child-care expenses exceed $5,000 per year, you can set aside up to $5,000 in pretax money in your FSA, then claim the dependent-care credit for up to $1,000 in additional expenses.

Talk to your tax professional to get the most benefit.

Earned Income Tax Credit

Another common tax credit is the Earned Income Tax Credit (EITC). The EITC is a refundable credit. That means, if you qualify for this credit, you get the full credit regardless of how much tax you owe. This credit, too, has been extended for the five years.

The key words to this credit are earned income.

That means a job, that you are working. If you are low income, and have income that you earned from working, check into the requirements for this credit. You do not have to have a child to qualify for this credit. You just have to have earned income. You get more credit for kids though.

The basic rules for this credit are:

✔ Must have a valid Social Security Number.

✔ You must have earned income from employment or from self-employment.

✔ Your filing status cannot be married filing separately.

✔ You must be a U.S. citizen or resident alien all year, or a nonresident alien married to a U.S. citizen or resident alien and filing a joint return.

✔ You **cannot** be a qualifying child of another person.

✔ If you do not have a qualifying child, you must:
   o be age 25 but under 65 at the end of the year,
   o live in the United States for more than half the year, and
   o not qualify as a dependent of another person.

The income requirements for tax year 2013:

Tax Year 2013 Income Limits and Range of EITC			
Number of Qualifying Children	For Single/Head of Household or Qualifying Widow(er), Income Must be Less Than	For Married Filing Jointly, Income Must be Less Than	Maximum EITC
No Child	$14,340	$19,680	$487
One Child	$37,870	$43,210	$3,250
Two Children	$43,038	$48,437	$5,372
Three or More Children	$46,227	$51,567	$6,044

Go to www.irs.gov to check the dollar amounts for each year, or if you have questions. Credits can be tricky to understand. Sometimes the IRS gets a little long-winded in their explanations. Ask an advisor or call the toll-free IRS number or take advantage of any free local tax help. There are many community organizations that offer free tax help each tax season. Check to see where you have this in your community. If you are not sure, call the IRS and ask if there are any VITA sites in your area. VITA is Volunteer Income Tax Assistance.

Many people are entitled to this EITC and do not claim it. If you want to read more, get IRS Publication 596.

After you know you qualify for EITC, you have two choices for figuring the credit:

Have the IRS figure the credit for you or figure the credit yourself.

If you have the IRS compute it: Follow the instructions for Line 64a on Form 1040, Line 38a on Form 1040A, or line 8a on Form 1040EZ.

Figure the credit yourself: To do this you must use the Earned Income Credit Worksheet (EIC Worksheet) in the instruction booklet for Form 1040, Form 1040A, or Form 1040EZ, and the Earned Income Credit (EIC) Table in the instruction booklet, or use the EITC Assistant Tool online. It is available in both English and Spanish.

If you qualify for the EITC, you may also be entitled to a similar credit on your state tax return. Many, but not all, states allow an earned income tax credit on the state return, too. Ask your tax advisor or check online. About half the states currently allow this credit. To see what your state offers, visit http://www.

taxcreditsforworkingfamilies.org/earned-income-tax-credit/states-with-eitcs/.

There is one more thing you need to know about EITC. You can get a little advance credit in your paycheck throughout the year instead of waiting for the tax return to be filed to claim the credit then. This is called Advance Earned Income Tax Credit.

To get the Advance Earned Income Tax Credit, there is a form you fill out and give to your employer if you expect to qualify and have at least one child. Your employer gives a portion in each paycheck.

A little extra in the paycheck is a nice option if you want to take advantage of it. When you file your tax return at the end of the year, report the amount of the credit you have already received (it will be on your W-2 earnings statement from your employer) and file for the rest of the credit due you.

Visit http://www.irs.gov/Individuals/EITC,-Earned-Income-Tax-Credit,-Questions-and-Answers for all the detailed info on the Earned Income Tax Credit.

Child & Dependent Care

Another common credit is the Credit for Child and Dependent Care Expenses. If you have kids under age thirteen and pay child care expenses so you can go to work, you may be able to claim this credit. If you also have to pay someone to care for your spouse or your dependent who cannot care for himself/herself while you go to work, you may be entitled to this credit as well.

The credit is 20% to 35% of those expenses that you pay. For all the details, see Publication 503 or www.irs.gov.

The same kind of rules for "qualifying" children apply here, too. In general, if you work and pay day care, this credit is for you. You will have to identify the caregiver on the form and give the social security number if you pay an individual or tax ID number if you use a day care center.

Paying a babysitter while you work, or look for work, counts. Follow the instructions for Form 2441 and it walks you through to easily compute the credit.

The credit varies from person to person because it is based on what you pay for child care and what your earned income is. For example, if you pay $3,000 for day care and your income is over $43,000, you can get 20% of the $3,000 as your credit. That's $600.

This credit allows working parents—or those looking for work—to report up to $3,000 of child care-related expenses per child, up to a maximum of $6,000 per family. Families can receive up to 35% of their expenses as a credit, with lower-income families receiving the highest percentages.

> Families can receive up to 35% of their expenses as a credit...

Should the tax breaks have expired, the credit would have reverted back to prior rules where parents could only report up to $2,400 per child or $4,800 per family, and families received a maximum credit of just 30% of expenses.

That would mean the biggest credit that parents with two children could receive would be $1,440, compared to a $2,100 credit under the current tax code. The current code was extended for this credit permanently.

Education

Other loved credits are Education Tax Credits. These tax credits can help offset the costs of higher education for you or your dependent. Schooling is not cheap and you need every break that comes your way.

If you or your student is enrolled at least half time, check out these credits.

Check with your tax advisor as to what Education Tax Credits are in and what are out. There are always changes afoot.

Introduced as part of Obama's stimulus plan, the American Opportunity Tax Credit aimed to help lower-income families pay for college. It replaced the Hope Credit and allows qualifying families to claim up to $2,500 each year for four years.

Obama made the credit 40% refundable, meaning a family that qualifies for the full $2,500 can receive $1,000 of the credit in cash and the rest must be applied toward their tax liability.

That refundable $1,000 is especially important for low-income families, since they often don't have big enough tax bills to apply a non-refundable credit. Often, the refundable amount is the only portion they receive.

But as we go to press, the American Opportunity Tax Credit was scheduled to disappear at the end of the year and the education credit will revert back to the Hope Credit.

The Hope Credit applies for the first two years of college or vocational school. The credit can be up to $1,800 per student per year. This credit is not refundable. You only get the credit for two years, not four, like the American Opportunity Tax Credit.

Good news. The last minute deal to avert the so-called "fiscal cliff" saved the American Opportunity Credit and extended it for five more years. Part of the 2009 stimulus bill, this American Opportunity Tax Credit allows middle- and low-income families a tax deduction of up to $2,500 a year in education expenses for four years. A total credit of $10,000 is a good credit and many folks are glad it was saved.

> ...allows qualifying families to claim up to $2,500 each year...

If you have gone back to school and also have a kid in college, you are allowed to get double dips, meaning you both qualify.

Watch the income limits, however. If you are married filing jointly and your income is over certain amounts, you do not get these education credits. If your income is between certain amounts, the amount of the credit is reduced.

Check www.irs.gov for current limits, as they adjust ever year.

To get the full scoop, check out www.irs.gov or get Publication 970. The form to claim these credits is Form 8863.

FYI: All forms and publications for all credits are available for download and printing at www.irs.gov.

Savers

One credit that not many folks know about is called the Saver's Credit. The purpose of this credit is to help workers save for retirement and get a tax break now. If you put money into an IRA (Individual Retirement Account) or your employer's 401(k) plan, this Saver's Credit may apply to you.

This credit is in addition to the other tax benefits for saving in a retirement account. If you qualify, a Saver's Credit can reduce or even eliminate your tax bill.

Depending on your adjusted gross income and tax filing status, you can claim the credit for 50%, 20% or 10% of the first $2,000 you contribute during the year to a retirement account. Therefore, the maximum credit amounts that can be claimed are $1,000, $400 or $200.

The biggest credit amount a married couple filing jointly can claim together is $2,000. But if you and/or your spouse took a taxable distribution from your retirement account during the two years prior to the due date for filing your return (including extensions), that distribution reduces the size of the Saver's Credit available to you.

The Saver's Credit is non-refundable. It can reduce the tax you owe to zero, but it can't provide you with a tax refund.

Currently, the maximum adjusted gross income for Saver's Credit eligibility is $59,000 in 2013 for a married couple filing jointly, $44,250 in 2013 for a head of household, and $29,500 in 2013 for all other taxpayers. The maximum credit you can claim phases out as your income increases.

2012 Adjusted Gross Income:

Credit	Single Filer	Head of Household	Joint Filers
50%	$17,250 or less	$25,875 or less	$34,500 or less
20%	$17,251-$18,750	$25,876-$28,125	$34,501-$37,500
10%	$18,751-$28,750	$28,126-$43,125	$37,501-$57,500

These numbers adjust each year, but if you are in the general range, ask your tax preparer about the Saver's Credit. A 2010 survey showed that only about 12% of the population in this income range had even heard of the credit.

If you have tax credits available to you—free money!—take them!

This credit is aimed to encourage folks to save for retirement. The credit amount is based on filing status, adjusted gross income, tax liability, and amount contributed to qualifying retirement programs. Form 8880 is used to claim the Saver's Credit, and the instructions have details on how to figure the credit.

Begun in 2002 as a temporary provision, the Saver's Credit was made a permanent part of the tax code in legislation enacted in 2006. To help preserve the value of the credit, income limits are now adjusted annually to keep pace with inflation. More information about the credit, and all credits, is at www.irs.gov.

With all the ways that the government puts the screws to us, tax credits are one way we can collect a little something back from the government. If you qualify for a tax credit, file your form and claim it! You could of course, let that money go to the US Treasury. Shouldn't it go in your pocket instead?

Pay attention to what gets you the biggest bang for the buck. If your employer offers an FSA (Flexible Spending Plan), use it. That usually is the best way to maximize your tax dollars.

There are a large number of employers out there that offer the FSA plan. If you can pay your child care expenses with pre-tax money, why not?

The employer takes money out of your paycheck each week that goes toward your day care provider expenses. You do not have to pay tax on this portion of your income. That means big savings at the end of the year.

Many employers offer this same kind of plan for your health and medical expenses. You predict how much you pay during the year for insurance and doctor bills and prescriptions. The employer withholds that from your paycheck and puts it into a spending account. You pay for your doctor bills and pharmacy costs with this money.

Some companies call them cafeteria plans; some call them flexible spending accounts. Talk to the human resource person at your place of employment to see what is offered and all of the terms and conditions.

When it comes to daycare options, explore all your choices. Some employers provide day care onsite. If there is a fee for that, it can be part of the FSA money or you can use it as money you pay to compute the child tax credit. Usually, it's best to use FSA first.

Depending on your income level, there is a program called Head Start that provides free preschool for families who qualify. Head Start provides lower income families with the tools to help the development of their children. The program offers a variety of educational, social, and health services.

These kids get help when they are young. They can then head off to kindergarten and elementary school with the skills to keep up with all the others kids. The program likes to think of itself as giving children a "head start" on the path toward success. There are also programs now called Even Start that provide the same goals. Go to the web for more information: http://www.acf.hhs. gov/programs/ohs/.

Adoption

Another IRS credit on the chopping block is Adoption Tax Credit. It's been around for fifteen years to help families who adopt cover some of that expense. If the fiscal cliff happens, this credit is gone. Only families who adopt a special needs child will be able to claim a credit under the new rules. That credit is limited to $6,000, based on expenses for families who adopt special needs children in foster care.

Nearly 100,000 people used the Adoption Tax Credit. There are that many children waiting in foster homes, who are not special needs kids, who may not get adopted if the credit goes away.

One organization is fighting to save this credit. You can read more at http://adoptiontaxcredit.org/faqs/.

Adoption is very expensive. With or without tax credits, if you plan on adoption, you need to know that there are benefits available. The National Adoption Foundation gives financial assistance. They provide grants, not only to be used toward adopting a child, but toward raising a child as well. Learn more at: www.nafadopt.org.

> ...you need to know there are benefits available.

Some employers and companies today offer adoption benefits to their employees to help ease the burden of the large costs associated with adoption. Check with your employer to find out what your company is offering. If you are planning to adopt, and your company does not have an adoption benefits program, talk to them about implementing one. As I have said over and over again, all you have to do is ask.

The government does have tax credits, and they also have assistance programs. Don't forget to take advantage of what our government has to offer. If you are in need, use whatever aid you can.

If you find yourself in crisis, there are agencies and organizations that provide assistance when crisis hits. If you need money to get by or to pay the bills, pay the rent or pay to get the car fixed, whatever you may need, there are places that can offer you help.

The U.S. Department of Health and Human Services (DHHS) is a good place to start. Operating in ten regions across the country, the DHHS has the goal of maintaining the "health and well-being" of our nation.

DHHS offices vary from region to region, so be sure to check what is available where you live. In the Seattle region, for example, DHHS offers three different kinds of emergency grants. They work with other agencies and organizations to provide housing, medical aid, food, and clothing.

For more information or to find your region, visit www.dhhs.gov.

The Community Action Partnership is another emergency needs provider. This partnership oversees a network of Community Action Agencies all over the country. These agencies are nonprofit organizations that provide support and financial assistance to low-income families.

They offer community outreach, job training, counseling, food pantries, and transportation programs. To learn more about this network, check them out at: www.communityactionpartnership.com.

Government Benefits

And once again, you can go to http://www.benefits.gov/ to learn more about a whole host of emergency grants. If an emergency strikes and you need help, you can also call local agencies where you can get the number right out of your phone book.

For food and shelter needs, contact the local Salvation Army or your local Red Cross chapter. To learn more, you can go to: www. salvationarmy.org.

Don't forget that your local Public Assistance office may be able to provide the funds that you need. If you need aid, apply for it. In some states, Pubic Aid will offer assistance while you are waiting to receive funds from other grant programs. The amount that is provided differs in each state. Check with your local office when you need help.

For folks over the age of 65 who struggle to pay for Medicare coverage, if you have income from working, you may qualify for assistance programs even if your income is higher than the income limits.

If you qualify for a QMB, SLMB, or QI program, you automatically qualify to get extra help paying for Medicare prescription drug coverage, too. There are four programs:

✔ Qualified Medicare Beneficiary (QMB) Program

✔ Specified Low-Income Medicare Beneficiary (SLMB) Program

✔ Qualifying Individual (QI) Program

✔ Qualified Disabled and Working Individuals (QDWI) Program

The QDWI program helps pay the Part A premium. You may qualify if any of these apply to you:

✔ You're a working disabled person under 65

✔ You lost your premium-free Part A when you went back to work

✔ You aren't getting medical assistance from your state

✔ You meet the income and resource limits required by your state

QMB is Qualified Medicare Beneficiary, a program aimed toward easing the burden of Medicare payments. It's simple to apply for. If you qualify, the benefits are good. They provide payments toward Medicare Part A and Medicare Part B.

For more info on these programs, call Medicare at 1-800-MEDICARE (1-800-633-4227), or visit their site at: www.medicare.gov, and http://www.medicare.gov/your-medicare-costs/help-paying-costs/medicare-savings-program/medicare-savings-programs.html.

There are countless state and local programs out there that offer help, too. Check with your local Family Assistance Administration office (FAA). For example, in Arizona, the FAA administers the Arizona Cash Assistance Program.

This program gives debit cards that work just like cash. Use at ATMs and in most stores. The cash is not debited out of your account, but the cash assistance account. For more info, see http://www.benefits.gov/benefits/benefit-details/1048.

Check out http://www.benefits.gov/ (type in the name of the program, Family Assistance Administration, or your state name followed by cash assistance program, in the search box) to see if you are eligible and to get more information on program requirements and contact information.

Don't forget about unemployment benefits. If you become among the millions of laid off workers, the first thing you need to do is contact your state unemployment office and file for unemployment.

Every state offers unemployment insurance and you need to take advantage. Apply with your state local office. This is income that you get and do not have to repay. Look at it like a grant from a program that wants to kick-start your life. The amount you get is based on past wages and your particular state's rules. Each state has a cap. For more information, type in "unemployment benefits" and your state name.

No matter what you have going on, reach out for whatever funds the government has available. Use them. This is your country. You are a tax-paying citizen. Exercise your rights to use the benefits available to you.

What do you need?

Are you in need of afterschool care or caring for elderly parents? Try www.salvationarmyusa.org or www.catholiccharitiesusa.org.

Are you a senior citizen in need of assistance with meals? Tryhttp://www.fns.usda.gov/programs-and-services .

Are you in need of meal assistance for your children at school? Tryhttp://www.fns.usda.gov/nslp/national-school-lunch-program .

For funds for senior citizens to buy at local farmers markets, tryhttp://www.fns.usda.gov/sfmnp .

Are you buying a home in a rural area? Try www.rurdev.usda.gov.

Are you a senior citizen wanting to learn about a reverse mortgage on your house, where it pays you every month? Try www. ftc.gov.

Are you a college student? Try www.ed.gov/or www.studentaid. ed.gov.

Do you want to continue on with your education? Tryhttp:// www.aauw.org/what-we-do/educational-funding-and-awards/ .

Do you want to learn a foreign language? Tryhttp://www2. ed.gov/about/offices/list/ope/iegps/index.html .

This should give you an idea of what is out there. Ask around. Search the internet. These web site addresses were accurate as of press time and most are agencies that will continue to be around for a long time. Changes in actual grant amounts or qualifications may occur every year. Agencies are constantly amending their programs, so do the research. You'll see what is out there right now and find something that sparks your interest.

> The web is the best source for quick and easy access to all this free money.

If you do not have the internet at your house, go to your local library. The web is the best source for quick and easy access to all this free money.

For the directory of federal government agencies, you can visit http://www.usa.gov/ or 1-880-FED-INFO.

Detailed grant information is printed in hard copy in the Catalog of Federal Domestic Assistance and is available for just over $100. You can order it from the US Government Bookstore at http://bookstore.gpo.gov/. Let me warn you, this book is 2,400 pages!

You now understand that there are more programs and more ways to get money to help your financial situation. Stay informed and stay on top of your debt. Using the government is a great cure.

CHAPTER 22

Free Money

"There's no such thing as a free lunch."

Maybe there's not such a thing as a free lunch, but we've discovered a lot of ways to free money. You can, too. Our readers have.

Veronica S. received over $28,000 in free money. She states: *"I didn't have to pay it back. It's my money. And, I was able to pay off my debt and now I feel free."*

Feeling free is exactly what you want.

The first *Debt Cures* book launched my quest to find sources of free money for you, and it even spawned a book, too, Kevin Trudeau's Free Money They Don't Want You to Know About, because we found so much information. Do you have that book?

There are many sources of free money, including countless grants and loans available from the government and private foundations. Free funds from the feds is, especially, what we love to share with you.

If you want to stay up to date on all the Free Money sources, subscribe to that monthly newsletter, too. We keep you current as information is always changing and more sources are always becoming available. Call and sign up for that, too, plus the *Debt Cures* newsletter.

To get started with just a teaser of all the free money sources, let's begin with our love/hate relationship with the federal government. They drive me crazy and then they have some good stuff for folks, too. Like grants.

Government grants

The first site to check out online is www.benefits.gov/. There is over $400 billion in grant money that gets awarded to people just like you. Repeat: $400 BILLION.

That's a lot of free money.

This is a great site to find grants and assistance. There are literally thousands of government programs available and most people have no idea that they even exist. Now you do. Take a click and see what you think.

You do not have to give your confidential, private information, but by filling out a short survey, you can learn what kinds of programs are available to you. Navigating this site is easy and an immense time saver.

Trying to research each grant independently would be maddening. To have a "one-stop shopping" sort of site is very helpful.

You can use the Quick Search feature. Click on a topic; grants and programs in that category are listed. Some of the categories include:

- ✔ Awards
- ✔ Counseling
- ✔ Disaster Relief

✔ Financial Assistance

✔ Grants, Scholarships, Fellowships

✔ Housing

✔ Loans

✔ Social Security/Pension

✔ Child Care

✔ Disability Assistance

✔ Education

✔ Food

✔ Health Care

✔ Insurance

✔ Medicare

✔ Utilities

That should give you an indication of the vastness of this site and of federal government programs. A million people every year get money from the government, either through grants or loans.

Read that again: A million people every year get money from the government, from these kinds of programs.

Were you even aware of that?

Now you know.

And, it could be you.

By answering a few brief questions, you can find out if you are eligible for any grants or loans or assistance programs.

Hundreds of programs

There are hundreds of grant programs from twenty-six different government agencies on this site. It certainly may be worth a few minutes of your time to take a look for yourself.

There are two ways to navigate this site. Let's assume you have no idea what you might qualify for or what you are looking for specifically. Most people are like that. Click on the "Start Here" button.

The next screen is an easy-to-answer list of 40+ questions. Don't worry, it will take you only five to ten minutes to complete. The questions are simple and straightforward, and completely anonymous. You do not give your name or social security number. The only personal questions are age, gender, and income level.

After you answer the questions, a list of possible grant or benefit programs pops up that you could be eligible for—how simple is that?!

> ...might surprise you to find all the programs you can apply to.

We know a man who was questioning whether or not he could qualify for any grants. After all, he's a millionaire. Aren't these grants only for "poor" people? He qualified for seven grants! If he can do it, so can you.

The search engine built in to this web site is a great tool. Take some time to do your own search and it just might surprise you to find all the programs you can apply to. The web saves hours upon countless hours of time and frustration when it comes to locating possible money sources.

The next site to check out is www.grants.gov/.

This is another amazing website for government grants. To just browse through all the information, registration is not required. If you want to apply for a grant, you will have to register. (It's free.)

SBA

The Small Business Administration (SBA) has many wonderful programs that you can explore. They give out grants as well as loans. The loans often have super terms and incredible interest rates; SBA loans can usually beat any bank in town. Although it is a loan and you will have to repay, it is a sensational deal, and again, worth checking out.

For a quick link, try www.sba.gov/services.

The SBA also has women's business centers. The Small Business Association's Office of Women's Business Ownership focus is to help women achieve their dreams and improve their communities by providing assistance for starting a business.

The SBA provides training on how to get started and how to maintain a successful business, and they provide assistance as you go. Check out the SBA's website for all the details at http://www.sba.gov/about-offices-content/1/2895. The SBA's Women's Business Center Program comprises a national network of WBCs providing business training, counseling and other resources to help women start and grow successful businesses. Click on the link to go to your state www.sba.gov/about-offices-content/1/2895#.

SBA's Women's Business Centers (WBC) provide resource centers across the nation to help women get their businesses launched and to be available for guidance every step of the way. Grants are available for five years, with the option to renew for another five years. The program's mission is to "level the playing field." These grants are offered to new businesses and existing businesses looking to expand.

The next site to check out is www.usa.gov. The official website of the federal government, USA.gov, also contains valuable information about all US government agencies and their various grants.

Click on Benefits and Grants. This link gives you information on grants, loans, financial aid and other benefits. You can even sign up to be notified when the benefit page is updated.

Loans

www.govloans.gov is another federal government site focusing on loan information, not grants. It is an excellent source for locating available loans for children, agriculture, business, disaster relief, education, housing, veterans, or just about anything for which you might need a loan.

www.grantsolutions.gov is another site to try. This is the web address for the Grants Center of Excellence (COE), a partnership between agencies within Health and Human Services, Department of Agriculture, the Denali Commission, and Department of Treasury. The COE states that these partner agencies distribute over $250 billion in grants each year.

The Women's Financial Fund offers business grants of up to $5,000. They do not look at your credit report. Their website explains that the money is a grant and not a loan, therefore, your ability to pay it back is not an issue.

Getting a grant is a great way to launch your dreams. Visit their web site at www.womensbusinessgrants.com/who.shtml.

Another opportunity for women is at www.count-me-in.org with info on loan programs, scholarships, and women-in-business loans. Also see:www.fundsnetservices.com/searchresult/15/Women-Grants.html; or www.womensnet.net; plus a host of others.

Besides government grants, there are foundations with money to give away. That is the whole purpose of their existence. If they exist just to give funds, don't you want to be on the list of possible contenders?

Do your research and see if you qualify. There are thousands of grants and each has its own set of requirements. Doing a little window shopping on the foundations is very interesting. You may come across something that fits you or maybe you'll find something for someone you know.

> ...private sources can often be a terrific source of funds.

Some sites worth your time:

✔ www.foundationcenter.org/getstarted/individuals/
✔ www.fundsnetservices.com
✔ www.foundations.org

I am a big believer in foundations, and these private sources can often be a terrific source of funds. The sites listed above are just an example of what is out there.

Private foundations, government (all levels: federal, state, county, and local) and corporations all have grant money and assistance loans that they want to give away. They want to give it away!

All you need to do is apply.

Only apply for the ones that you are eligible for, of course. If the grant is for a salmon fisherman in Alaska and you are not a salmon fisherman in Alaska, you won't get the grant so don't waste anyone's time. Go find the grants for a photographer in Virginia, or female business owner, or rural homeowner, or whatever, and apply for what you qualify for.

You have nothing to lose. Ask and you just may receive.

Education grants

There are many grant opportunities for those pursuing higher education. Some grants are for traditional college age students, and others are not. If getting your education has been your dream, go find a grant!

If you think that you can't afford college, think again. There is probably a program for you. Check out these sites:

- ✔ www.studentaid.ed.gov
- ✔ www2.ed.gov/programs/iegpsirs/index.html
- ✔ www2.ed.gov/about/offices/list/fsa/index.html
- ✔ www2.ed.gov/about/offices/list/ope/iegps/index.html

Many students long to study abroad. There are many grants, scholarships, and fellowships available.

- ✔ www.studyabroadfunding.org/
- ✔ FederalFundingPrograms.org
- ✔ IIEPassport.org
- ✔ http://allabroad.us/funding-study-abroad-scholarships.php
- ✔ http://www.studyabroad.com/scholarships.aspx

You also need to be aware that there are grant and loan programs to help with paying utility bills, child care, and grocery bills. There are organizations that give such "emergency" money. It can help you to bridge the gap to use this assistance, and to help keep your monthly expenditures under control.

Don't forget about these options and don't be too proud to take advantage of all that is available. The programs exist. Use them!

Social Security

If you are disabled or if you are a senior citizen, Social Security has a branch that can help you. Funded by the general tax coffers, Supplemental Security Income (SSI) exists to aid seniors, the blind, and the disabled in paying off their everyday expenses.

Blind and disabled children can apply as well. It is an income-based program. The less income you have, the more aid you can qualify for. If you are eligible, fill out an application. You can use these dollars to pay off your bills.

The SSI sends out checks every month to help people pay off their expenses. They dole out thousands of dollars a year. Now isn't that worth knowing? Even if you don't qualify, maybe you know someone who does. Share what you know.

Call Social Security at 1-800-772-1213 to see if you meet the current income requirements. You can also learn more and apply at: www.socialsecurity.gov/ssi/text-understanding-ssi.htm.

The monthly benefit rates change each year. Some states will even add to the federal benefits that SSI is already giving. So, do the research for your state, too. If you qualify for SSI, you may also qualify for certain additional services within your state, too.

State programs

State governments have many programs that exist to give you a helping hand. For example, many states have programs to help pay utilities.

Arizona Public Service (APS) has a program that helps low-income residents pay their energy bills. Qualified individuals can get a discount of up to 40% off. They look at your household income and how much energy you use to calculate what you pay. The savings on your energy costs can give you money to use to pay off loans or credit cards.

For more information, visit www.aps.com.

Many states do have similar programs. Whatever state you live in, research the programs that are available to you.

There are also federally funded energy assistance programs. The Low Income Home Energy Assistance Program (LIHEAP), run by the Division of Energy Assistance, is a great place to go if you're looking for some funds to pay your energy bills. Their program's dollars are distributed among all fifty states. Check to see if you can qualify within your state. Get more information here: http://liheap.org/.

Besides energy bills, you have other utilities that need to be paid. Your state may offer an assistance program. Pick up the phone and ask. I know you have learned by now that great and surprising things come to those who ask.

Call the utility office in your state. You never know—you may be able to receive significant discounts on all your utilities.

There are a number of programs available to help you with child care expenses. Anyone with children knows how expensive day care can be. When the kids start school and the parent no longer has to pay the large day care bill every month, there is a large boost to the monthly income. Think if you could get some assistance now to boost your income.

The Office of Family Assistance (OFA) operates the Temporary Assistance for Needy Families (TANF) program. This program has been in existence since 1997. It provides free job training and education, and helps with locating grants that pay for child care. Visit www.acf.hhs.gov/programs/ofa/programs/tanf for more info.

By contacting state agencies, the OFA can find a program that is right for you. You can learn more at: www.acf. hhs.gov/programs/ofa/. Also, be sure to check out some other opportunities at: www.childcareaware.org or www. theworkfamilyconnection.org.

> ...funds to pay your energy bills...help you with child care expenses.

Working parents have so much to juggle and the stress level can get so high. Find out all your options and pursue them. If there is cash available, don't you want it to be yours?

Families

The U.S. Department of Health and Human Services is responsible for another organization that may be able to help you. The Child Care and Development Block Grant (CCDBG) provides funds to assist with child care costs as well.

Visit the Afterschool Alliance for more info at http://www. afterschoolalliance.org/PolicyEconRecovCCDBG.cfm.

Every year, families can receive up to thousands of dollars to pay their day care costs. Parents are allowed to choose their own child care provider, as long as it is a legal operation and it meets all state health and safety requirements.

The recurring theme throughout all my books, seminars, and teaching is that you must act. Learning that grants are available is good. Applying for grants is even better.

Fill out the applications and send them off. Many are able to be done via the internet. It's quick and it's free and it's immediate.

When you are writing your grant application, be yourself and be passionate. Don't try to sound like anything different than who you are.

Grants usually have to be straight to the point and not very wordy. There are people who specialize in writing grants. If you need help, contact the agency directly or hire a grant writer, if the amount is enough to warrant paying for that service. Most of the time you can follow the directions and do it all yourself.

YOU can be among the million

A million people every year get money from the government, either through grants or loans. A MILLON PEOPLE.

Did you have any idea there was that much money available and that there were that many different programs? There may be something out there for you.

Read about grants and low cost loans. Ask people. Surf the internet. A little information can take you a very long way.

There are hundreds and thousands of programs offered every year. Some have specific restrictions as to how you must spend the money; some do not. Getting the money could even be easier than you would expect. Phone calls and filling out applications are usually all it takes.

Some grants require lots of paperwork, but you can find grants that merely require an easy-to-complete form with information you already know. Whatever office is giving the grant can answer any of your questions. They are happy to work with you.

There are many specific, more narrow grants as well, and there are places that exist simply to offer a helping hand. Perhaps you find yourself in a position where you are now looking for work and you do not have appropriate clothes. Most every state has a program like www.dressforsuccess.org and www.bottomlesscloset.org that can provide you with interview outfits and the clothes are yours to keep.

Organizations like that are tremendous. They discovered a need and filled it. And also what I find fulfilling is how a local community program can become a national force. There is power in good deeds.

Other sources

Another little known source of free money is the class action lawsuit. You may be party to some money and not be aware of it. For example, maybe your utility company mischarged for years. A class action lawsuit can be brought against the company.

That means not one person is suing, but the suit is filed on behalf of everyone it affects. Everyone who paid their bills during that timeframe of the overcharges is entitled to a refund of these charges in the class action suit.

There are suits being filed all the time and you may be included. When you get a letter in the mail that says you are part of a class action suit, do not toss it in the trash. There usually is a short form to fill out and return. What have you got to lose?

The settlement portion that comes your way could be a few bucks, or it could be big bucks!

Instead of waiting for a letter to appear in your mailbox, you can actively search class action suits that might pertain to you.

Visit www.topclassactions.com to see what is currently going on and what has been settled.

Besides the government programs and all that is mentioned above, there are foundations that exist to help people who need money. Research and apply. Here are just some of the private foundations that give personal and business grants:

- ✔ Wheless Foundation, P.O. Box 1119, Shreveport, LA 71152

- ✔ Simon & Schwab Foundation, P.O. Box 1014, Columbus, GA 31902

- ✔ Coulter Foundation, P.O. Box 5247, Denver, CO 80217

- ✔ Thatcher Foundation, P.O. Box 1401, Pueblo, CO 81002

- ✔ Biddle Foundation, Inc., 61 Broadway, Room 2912, New York, NY 10006

- ✔ Avery-Fuller Children Center, 251 Kearney Street, No. 301, San Francisco, CA 94108

- ✔ Jane Nugent Cochems Trust, c/o Colorado National Bank of Denver, P.O. Box 5168, Denver, CO 80217

- ✔ Unocal Foundation, P.O. Box 7600, Los Angeles, CA 90051

- ✔ Wal-Mart Foundation, 702 Southwest 8th Street, Bentonville, AK 72716

- ✔ The Piton Foundation, 370 17th St., Ste 5300, Denver, CO 80202

- ✔ Frank R. Seaver Trust, 714 W. Olympic Boulevard, Los Angeles, CA 90015

- ✔ Earl B. Gilmore Foundation, 160 S. Fairfax Avenue, Los Angeles, CA 90036

- ✔ The Commonwealth Fund, One East 75th Street, New York, NY 10021-2692

- ✔ The Cullen Foundation, P.O. Box 1600, Houston, TX 77251

- ✔ The James Irvine Foundation, One Market Plaza, San Francisco, CA 94105

- ✔ William Penn Foundation, Two Logan Square, 11th floor, 100 N. 18th Street, Philadelphia, PA 19103

- ✔ Blanchard Foundation, c/o Boston Sake, One Boston Place, Boston, MA 02106

- ✔ Xerox Foundation, P.O. Box 1600, Stamford, CT 06904

- ✔ Fairchild Industries, 20301 Century Boulevard, Germantown, MD 20874

- ✔ Charles and Els Bendheim Foundation, One Parker Plaza, Fort Lee, NJ 07024

- ✔ Blue Horizon Health & Welfare Trust, c/o Reid & Reige, Lakeville, CT 06039

- ✔ Broadcasters Foundation, Inc., 320 West 57th Street, New York, NY 10019

- ✔ Copley Fund, P.O. Box 696, Morrisville, VT 05661

- ✔ The Hawaii Foundation, 111 South King Street, P.O. Box 3170, Honolulu, HI 96802

- ✔ Inland Steel-Ryerson Foundation, 30 West Monroe Street, Chicago, IL 60603

- ✔ Northern Indiana Giving Program, 5265 Hohman Avenue, Hammond, IN 46320

- ✔ Cambridge Foundation, 99 Bishop Allen Drive, Cambridge, MA 02139

- ✔ Barker Foundation, P.O. Box 328, Nashua, NH 03301

- ✔ Morris Joseloff Foundation, Inc., 125 La Salee RD, W. Hartford, CT 06107

- ✔ Deposit Guaranty Foundation, P.O. Box 1200, Jackson, MS 39201

- ✔ Haskin Foundation, 200 E. Broadway, Louisville, KY 40202

- ✔ The Dayton Foundation, 1395 Winters Bank Tower, Dayton, OH 45423

- ✔ Ford Motor Company, The American Road, Dearborn, MI 48121

- ✔ Bohen Foundation, 1716 Locust Street, Des Moines, IA 50303

- ✔ Yonkers Charitable Trust, 701 Walnut Street, Des Moines, IA 50306

- ✔ Miles Foundation, P.O. Box 40, Elkhart, IN 46515

- ✔ Ametek Foundation, 410 Park Avenue, New York, NY 10022

- ✔ Horace B. Packer Foundation, 61 Main Street, Wellsboro, PA 16901

- ✔ John B. Lynch Scholarship Fund, P.O. Box 4248, Wilmington, DE 19807

- ✔ Camden Home for Senior Citizens, 66 Washington Street, Camden, ME 04843

- ✔ The Clark Foundation, 30 Wall Street, New York, NY 10005

- ✔ Richard & Helen DeVos Foundation, 7154 Windy Hill, SE, Grand Rapids, MI 49506

- ✔ Muskegon County Foundation, Fraunthal Center, Suite 304, 407 W. Western Avenue, Muskegon, MI 49440

- ✔ The H&R Block Foundation, 4410 Main Street, Kansas City, MO 64111

- ✔ New Hampshire Fund, One South Street, P.O. Box 1335, Concord, NH 03302-1335

- ✔ The Shearwater Foundation, Inc., c/o Alexander Nixon, 423 West 43rd Street, New York, NY 10036

Quite an impressive list, isn't it? Are you looking for medical or educational help? These foundations give grants for those areas:

- ✔ The Fasken Foundation, 500 West Texas Avenue, Suite 1160, Midland, TX, 79701

- ✔ The Rosario Foundation, 100 Broadway Avenue, Carnegie, PA 15106-2421

- ✔ Orange Memorial Hospital Corporation, P.O. Box 396, Orange, TX 77630

- ✔ The Perpetual Benevolent Fund, c/o Bay Bank Middlesex, 300 Washington St., Newton, MA, 02158.

- ✔ The Bagby Foundation for Musical Arts, 501 5th Ave., New York, NY 10017

- ✔ Larabee Fund Association, c/o Connecticut National Bank, 777 Main St., Hartford, CT 06115

- ✔ Battistone Foundation, P.O. Box 3858, Santa Barbara, CA 93103

- ✔ Avery-Fuller Children Center, 251 Kearney St., San Francisco, CA 94108

- ✔ Vero Beach Foundation for the Elderly, c/o First National Bank, 255 S. County Road, Palm Bch, FL 33480

✔ Smock Foundation, c/o Lincoln National Bank and Trust Co., P.O. Box 960, Fort Wayne, IN 46801

✔ Glifilin Memorial, Inc., W-555 First National Bank Building, St. Paul, MN, 55101

✔ Clarke Testamentary Trust/Fund Foundation, US National Bank of Oregon, P.O, Box 3168, Portland, OR, 97208

✔ Welsh Trust, P.O, Box 244, Walla Walla, WA 99362

Money can come from anywhere, at any time! Be on the lookout! This is a portion of what is available.

A word to the wise—also be on guard for websites that simply take your money and give you information that you could find for free yourself. There are web sites proclaiming free money sources and they want you to pay for a list. You can find the information yourself with a few clicks on the internet.

Sure, you can also pay a site to provide the listings for you. Simply know what you are paying for. It is ultimately up to you, but know that there are ways you can find free money and the cost to you is that too, free.

People have a hard time accepting that anything can be free. When we published the *Free Money* book, some people thought we, too, were scammers, that it could not be possible that the government was giving away all this money and not telling people about it. One blogger wrote in our defense: "There are a lot of programs out there that aren't advertised that the government does hide, and they are very hard to find on your own. His book reveals how and where to find them."

> You can find the information yourself with a few clicks on the internet.

Thank you.

This Free Money chapter is simply a bonus chapter to get your awareness up. Also, to increase your enthusiasm.

The more ways you can find to get money into your hands, the more power you feel. The more you build momentum. The more you feel confident and in control. That's a great way to cure your debt.

CHAPTER 23

Go and Do

"When the government violates the people's rights, insurrection is, for the people and for each portion of the people, the most sacred of the rights and the most indispensable of duties."
—Marquis de Lafayette

The government and the credit card companies certainly don't like me. I couldn't care less. They've been at me for years, probably always will be.

It is my right to speak up. It is our right to stick up for ourselves.

All I do is give you the information and the knowledge and the power to fight back. If they were not abusive, there would be no need for a fight.

Now, you have to fight the fight. You can read books all you want. I think you should read lots of books. Keep up to date. Stay informed. You also need to go and do something with that knowledge.

Knowledge is power only if you use it. If you know you should pick up the phone and call your credit card companies, but you don't do it, what's the point? How will anything change? The real cure to your debt is YOU!

I hope you feel armed and dangerous now, confident to tackle your debt and move on. Getting on with your life is freedom. Financial freedom opens doors. Financial freedom changes your life.

One thing you can do is call, e-mail, and write your elected officials. Many people do not know who their officials are or how to contact them. Look them up.

- ✔ www.senate.gov
- ✔ www.house.gov

Tell them what is on your mind. If you have a specific situation, inform them of your hardship. If you want to voice your support for credit card industry reform, do so. If you want to ask for legislation on a particular issue, do so.

You elected your senators and congressmen. They are supposed to be working for you. Let them know what you want. If you are angry, let them know. Be respectful, yet you can convey your frustration.

Use all the knowledge you now have.

This book is a guidebook, a playbook. Using the tips, techniques, methods, and plays included here, you can increase your credit score. Increasing that number affects all the numbers in your life. Upping that credit score gives your life a whole new perspective.

When your financial world falls right, it makes everything in your life seem better. Less stress can mean better health, better relationships, a better outlook.

Using the tips, techniques, methods, and plays included here, you can take your credit card payments and cut them way down,

maybe to half or less. Make those phone calls. Make those payments. Get better deals. Get better cards. Get rid of some of that
debt.

You can cut your debt in half. You can eliminate debt entirely.
Simply by using your smarts, your magic words, and *Debt Cures*
methods. Pay your mortgage in half the time. Pay your credit cards
in half the time. Get some items removed completely.

Using the tips, techniques, methods, and plays included here,
you can release old debt forever, you can eliminate it. Remember
all those magic words we discussed. Alleged Debt. Statute of
limitations. Identity Theft. Ask. Demand. Would you be willing.

Say please. Say thank you. Use all your magic words to open
doors and create a new financial reality. Shut the door on the stress
of the past. You do not have to keep living in worry and fear.

I want you to never feel the pressure of bill collectors ever again.
You do NOT have to take their garbage. They are not all-powerful.
YOU are.

Using the tips, techniques, methods, and plays included here,
you can implement debt cures and move forward in life. You are
smart. You are going to use your smarts from here forward.

Do not take the garbage. Do not accept the bull. Be a force in
your own world. You be the boss of your money.

Perhaps you will write in a success story. Open your eyes. Don't
forget about my friend who had $15,000 wiped away when he
realized the culprit, identity theft. Don't forget about all the people
who have tens of thousands of dollars of debt wiped away when
they realized it was old debt and it could not be collected. Take a
look at the table listing the Statute of Limitations (SOL) and you

will see that it does not take long for debt to be deemed old debt. Don't forget all the stories of folks who made phone calls and changed their bills and their lives.

Don't forget about all the people who now realized they had hope.

> ...there is always a way to make fast cash.

Words are powerful. Money talks. And, sometimes silence speaks louder. Never admit that a debt may be yours. Many times the debt collectors know that it is not your debt or that it is old debt and they come after you anyway. Keep quiet, use your magic words, and the debt and the debt collector can disappear.

Things are still crazy in our economy, no doubt about it. Maybe you are having trouble with the house payment. You can apply some of these techniques and get your home mortgage renegotiated. Maybe you just want to pay it off sooner. Done. You can do that without changing your monthly outlay. You can make money off of foreclosures and you can make money even if your own home is in foreclosure.

Don't forget all the ways to make fast money. No matter who you are or where you are, there is always a way to make fast cash. Some of these ways can become a business, too, if that is your desire. Now is a great time to go into business for yourself.

Take any one of these ideas in this book and apply it to your situation. I know these methods work. I know that you have the potential to save thousands of dollars. I get cards and letters that prove it.

You can be like Veronica S. who got over $28,000 in free money from the government. She said it was absolutely amazing.

Veronica agrees that many people think it's impossible to get money from the feds. She was successful getting her Free Money using the same methods we wrote about in the original *Debt Cures* book. "You just have to know where to look to get the information to be able to do it. It's possible. You just have to try. It was pretty simple. You just have to know what to do."

She's right. We can tell you to go look for unclaimed assets and missing tax returns, but if you do not do it, nothing will happen. If you do not put out any effort, nothing will happen. Don't you want something to happen?

Veronica was glad she pursued the tax refund tip.

Genesis and Elizabeth M. applied the same techniques I brought to you in the original *Debt Cures* book. They were able to negotiate their debt down and saved thousands of dollars.

Elizabeth states: "We negotiated our way through it with the banks. They didn't want to cooperate at first. We just kept pressing and pressing and negotiating. We brought our debt down from a big chunk, almost $30,000."

They are so glad they were persistent. "We weren't sleeping at night and we were stressed out. All that debt. So we decided to go for it. Talk to the banks. We figured we could be aggressive, just like they are. We got rid of all that debt and it was less than a year. You can do it yourself; you don't have to get a third party."

That's what we tell you. You can do this.

Elizabeth and Genesis were hesitant at first, but were tired of drowning in their debt. They figured they had nothing to lose.

She says: "We did it. No late fees, no interest payments and no bankruptcy. We are debt free. It was the most liberating day of our lives to be debt free. It's a freedom that you have inside of you."

Hearing from folks like this affirms that you can do it, too.

This couple said: "Well, we were able to get out of $30,000 in debt using the methods of the book, and if we could do it anybody can do it. It's something that everybody can do, definitely anybody."

Are you game?

You can be like Gina A. who got rid of $94,000 in debt. She applied the same method we brought you in the original *Debt Cures* book. She said the debt was weighing her down. Many people can relate. "Guilt, depression. It was the worst, I had so much debt I couldn't even put my kids into any dance classes or anything. It was crazy because I changed my cell number like three times because my phone was blowing up with all their calls, and the letters and mail and I didn't even want to go to my P.O. Box anymore because it was just nothing but bills. It was anxiety, a lot of anxiety. Definitely my blood pressure went up."

Gina liked the creative tips she learned. She challenged herself to get rid of her debt. "It was like going on a roller coaster ride, but you know every time I paid off a big chunk, I wanted to do it more. And I said, "OK, if I can get addicted to shopping I can get addicted to getting out of debt."

That is what she did. $94,000 worth of debt.

"The more I did it, it was monumental. Training my kids to do that is even bigger." Gina is right. We have to teach our kids the money basics.

Some things Gina did were basic, like no more shopping sprees. They would also set a family grocery budget and stick to it. "We eat everything by the end of the week and we don't buy anything. We call it eating out—of the cupboard. Really, those little things really, really helped."

Simple works. Gina loved all the "little tips" as she calls them and put them into practice. "The advice from that book really, really helped, so it was incredible. We're just trying to implement everything."

Gina cleaned out her closets and discovered she had a fortune in designer handbags. "I think I had every handbag. I sold everything, my Louis Vuitton's, my Juicy Couture's." The thrill of the cash was worth it.

Another Debt Cure that Gina loved was being able to stop the collection hounds. "One of my techniques was just communication and being real where I was at. They, the debt collectors, were able to work with us. And then for some bills, they said, "Well, since you've been working with us and you've been doing it in good faith, we'll cut it in half."

Cutting your debt in half simply by talking on the phone.

Gina explains: "People can't be afraid to talk to them. There was one credit card bill that was a couple thousand and they said if you just pay $400, we'll clear your debt."

Pay a little, get rid of a lot. It all adds up. In fact, it adds up to $94,000 of debt gone. Gina kept talking to all her creditors. She got interest rates lowered, she got debt eliminated. "They would waive late fees, they would delete amounts."

Having a plan, and acting on it, was all that it took. Bit by bit, piece by piece, Gina got rid of her debt and got her life back. "It was the most incredible feeling in my life and I just want that for everybody."

You can be like Al H. who cured $45,000 of debt. Al states: "I got in debt just being myself. Living my life day by day. One thing led to another and it started accumulating—and then high interest rates. One of the ways that creditors took advantage of me was charging me outrageous interest rates AND I was getting charged a daily overdraft fee. Another way creditors took advantage of me is that they continuously switch creditors. Once you start dealing with one creditor, then they end up transferring that debt to another creditor, then you start the whole process all over again."

Al continues: "I took an opportunity on a Bill Clinton scholarship to go study abroad at the American University in Dubai. When I was over there my bank started charging me a fee everyday while I was gone and I had no idea. My bank was charging me outrageous daily overdraft fees. So when I came back home18 months later, I had accrued an enormous amount of debt because they were charging me a daily overdraft fee for over eighteen months. I came home to $60,000 in debt."

We all know debt is stressful. "Being in debt is like the worst thing that could ever happen to me. I couldn't even get a rental car. Can't find a place to live. No places will even rent to you without having a good credit score. All my friends were starting families and buying houses…there's no chance I could purchase a home with being in the debt that I was in. It's really tough. Everyone else you know is out there making purchases and you can't. It just makes you feel like you're stuck in a stalemate when you're in debt. You can't move forward, like you have no future."

"I was constantly anxious and constantly nervous of how am I going to pay this. I started to get depressed. Debt starts to take a toll on your body, on your mind, on your spirit. I would go to bed at night and think about how much debt I had. Being in debt definitely impacted my relationships. I didn't really feel like going out on dates because I didn't feel like myself. I was stressed all the time. Being in debt is seriously like the worst thing that you can ever go through. Then you realize that the creditors have a way of manipulating the system and there is no recourse unless you know the tricks."

That's when Al got the *Debt Cures* book. He was skeptical, like many people. He said: "How's a book going to clear up my debt? If it was really such a thing, it would be all over every news outlet and all over in libraries and they would teach it in schools and it would be part of the curriculum in senior year in high school."

> Al started sticking up for himself and stopped feeling helpless.

Now that rings a bell.

Al started immediately getting to work using *Debt Cures* methods. "I've really been implementing all the tools inside the book. I've been sending letters, I've been making phone calls; I have really been reducing my debt overall. Using the methods in the book I was able to eliminate over $45,000 in debt. I was shocked at how quick I was able to eliminate my debt. I was surprised with this book. Someone in 8th grade can go through this whole book."

You don't have to be "educated" to implement these tips. Al started sticking up for himself and stopped feeling helpless. He started making money at what he is good at. "I'm a private swim instructor and life guard. I basically go to families' homes and do private swim instruction. Everything from stroke refinement, water safety, as well as competitive swimming. I do everything from children that are two years old that just want to get used to the water, do water safety, learn how to stay afloat, swim to the side of the pool to be safe, etc. to collegiate athletes who want stroke refinement and want to learn to become faster and be a more dominant swimmer."

If Al can get clients doing what he knows how to do, can't you find someone who needs your skills? You can make money in all kinds of creative ways.

He, too, is ecstatic. "There are no words to describe the way I feel being debt free. I mean I really feel like my life just started now. Being debt free is the best thing that could have happened to me. You know for the longest time I felt like I wasn't even being myself, like I was living in this bubble of debt. My life's changed now that I've gotten rid of debt because I can actually be myself again."

It's the little things that matter. Al explains it well: "One of the big benefits about being debt free is not feeling guilty about hanging out with friends, going out shopping, enjoying a coffee. Now that my debt is eliminated, I'm able to purchase a home, able to buy a car, able to go on vacations, able to treat my friends and family to dinner, and really just do anything I want now."

Do you long to be able to do what you want? You can. Start using these methods. Start making money and paying the debt and cutting the debt.

You can be like Ramanda S. who used to be stressed with debt and bills, and now has $300,000 worth of rental properties. Ramanda has come a long way and cashed in on many methods.

Finding lost money was a thrill: "You can look up your name, which I never knew, on the internet and get the money back. I got $350 on that one."

Ramanda also called in to stop having PMI payments on the mortgage when 20% equity was reached. "On the house payment, I saved a lot of money. They took that off and then I paid more on my principal and it took at least two years of interest off."

Heeding advice also works. Ramanda said that debt was stressing her out, so instead of freaking out about it, she simply took a second job waitressing and used that money to pay off the debt. "I felt better about myself because I paid it down, and really fast."

Ramanda was in banking, too. She saw right at the source how it was. "People who are in debt are always in need of another loan. They're going to need to pay their payments and if they can't pay their payments, the interest rate can go up for the bank. And that's why they like people in debt, because they have the highest rate."

She says: "I use my debt in a good way now. I don't close out credit cards anymore because that lowers your credit rating. So, now I hold onto them and they send me these checks that say you can have it free, for 0 percent. That's how I buy my properties. I'm fixing trailers and I have a whole year for free to pay."

Using the *Debt Cures* book, she eliminated $40,000 dollars in debt, "I was shocked to know that I could use debt in a good way."

"I was shocked when I realized that I could turn around and use those cards that I paid off that fast and that I could just use that debt at the 0% rate. I was shocked to find out that I could actually use debt to make money. Never even knew that was a possibility. I used my debt to start a real estate business. I make $35,000 alone on this house a year. I am able to use the techniques in the book to help me with that debt in a positive way, because now what I do when I buy something, I know how much the payment is going to be from the people who are going to live in it and I know when it's going to be paid back and I know exactly how long it's going to take me to pay it back."

I always tell folks it doesn't have to be hard. Ramanda agrees: "This is simple stuff to do. You don't have to be an expert, you don't have to have a degree. I'm very excited right now. I'm about to buy my next property. I'm now using my credit without laying out any money of my own to build my business. Without Kevin's book, I wouldn't have the financial freedom that I have today. I am very thankful that Kevin wrote that book."

Getting out of debt and turning the tables on the banks to make money yourself is freeing. "It feels so good to own a piece of property over $300,000. I only owe $50K on it. Now I know how to use my credit and I know how to use it in a good way instead of a bad way."

Ramanda said it best: "It is amazing to feel financially secure."

Do you want to feel financially secure? You can. You can be a success story, too.

Our economy is still in the toilet. The so-called recovery is taking its dear sweet time. We have four more years with the same president. The horizon looks pretty much the same. The feds may try to improve the situation, but usually their efforts end up with nothing really happening or things going from bad to worse.

Stay up to date with the latest ways to combat the times and situation. *Debt Cures* monthly newsletter is your next line of defense.

They—the banks, the credit card companies, the federal government—don't want you to know what is going on. They would prefer that you stayed in the dark, ignorant and uninformed.

They want your money. They don't want your complaints. Why should we care what they want?

It's your money. What do you want? You want to give it to them? You want to keep it for yourself?

Using these methods, you can do more of that. Go and do.

Thanks for reading.

—Kevin Trudeau